TENT LIFE

A beginner's guide to camping
and a life outdoors

DORON FRANCIS

Contents

Introduction

Being a Kiwi, the outdoors is practically in my blood. New Zealand is a small country but there's plenty of wilderness right on your doorstep – endless beaches, rivers and lakes, mountain ranges, untamed bushland and pristine forests. So is it any wonder that almost everyone is into some form of outdoor recreation – camping, surfing, biking, fishing, hunting, sailing and tramping (Kiwi name for hiking). I had a free-range childhood where we were always outside – exploring the local woodland, building camps, rafting in the creek and generally getting up to well-intentioned mischief.

When I was four my family moved to Great Britain. Like most people growing up at that time, international holidays were an almost unobtainable luxury. So my early camping experiences probably grew more out of necessity than from my parents' love of camping – let's face it, it's an inexpensive way to holiday with kids. I still remember the musty smell (aka the promise of adventure!) of our old canvas tent tied up with rope and stashed in the rafters of our garage. My parents would borrow bits and pieces of gear from neighbours and friends before we set off in our green Mini Cooper on camping trips to Cornwall or Scotland (I remember the rain well!).

The time my grandparents visited us in England is a favourite camping memory. The whole family squeezed into a pop-top Bedford campervan (which would later break down at many inconvenient times and locations!) for a six-month adventure around Europe. This was in a time long before the internet, so planning was fairly rough – a couple of borrowed guide books, maps, and advice from friends. Luckily, my grandad was an excellent resource when we got into trouble, as he had learnt fluent German, French and Italian as a prisoner of war in World War II.

Some of my first vivid memories are from this trip – touring through the French countryside, exploring the Swiss Alps, camping out on Italian and Spanish beaches, and making friends wherever we went. It was very basic living but we had a superb time. To this day our family still shares a love of the outdoors, and my mum is a grey nomad who lives in a converted bus on New Zealand's South Island.

Most of my fondest childhood memories are connected with the outdoors. These camping trips taught me about the value of being independent, and that setting off into the unknown was an effort that was mostly rewarded. Some of our best family experiences didn't cost the earth – making do with what you have can often result in the most joy and satisfaction.

Growing up in both New Zealand and England, I got to experience the different styles of camping and outdoor life. In England the wilderness was harder to find. Most camping involved orderly private campsites with tents lined up right next to each other in a nondescript field. While in New Zealand camping was done mostly in the 'bush' (back-country or wilderness), in national parks or on the beach. There we had untamed adventures with blazing campfires. We would fish or dive for mussels and paua (abalone) and tramp into the hills. Being less populated and urbanised than England, growing up in New Zealand meant that we had almost unlimited access to the land, which I loved, and is very much a luxury these days.

One of my first solo trips was travelling around Australia for a year when I was 18. Again, I was camping out of necessity (no money) while working seasonal jobs to pay for my trip. Throughout my twenties and early thirties, in between bouts of more serious jobs,

I dedicated my life to long trips to far-flung places, most notably South and Central America, Mexico, South-East Asia and India, where I spent a lot of my time trekking in mountains or forests.

In 2008, I moved to Australia where I met my wife, who is now the mother of our children. Together, we have been on some epic camping adventures. We've climbed volcanoes in Kamchatka in Far East Russia, camped in national parks in the United States, and tramped throughout New Zealand. In Australia, we've experienced hiking and 4WD trips to the Simpson Desert, Arnhem Land, the Flinders and MacDonnell Ranges, as well as plenty of simple camping trips closer to our home in Victoria. These experiences inspired us to start our own camping-related companies – Homecamp and Under Sky – both with a vision of encouraging people to spend more time in nature.

The world offers an open and inclusive invitation for everyone to enjoy nature's gifts and experience its transformative power. Camping allows us to intimately connect to the land, not just as an observer but also as a participant. It's an excellent gateway to begin your own love affair with the natural world. It's also a practical way to build confidence in your own self-sufficiency. I'm the first to admit that I'm no Bear Grylls, but you don't need to be.

At the time of writing, the world is in the middle of the COVID-19 global pandemic and Melbourne, where I live, is currently in our second lockdown of the year. Whatever your thoughts on this unprecedented crisis, there has never been a time in living memory where the liberties that we have always taken for granted have been so severely curtailed.

This new way of living has caused many people to reassess priorities and question the way we were living pre-COVID. The downtime of lockdowns around the world has resulted in new-found passions for cooking (social media feeds are full of everyone's freshly baked loaf of sourdough), spending quality time with family, and, of course, a new appreciation for the outdoors and breathing fresh air. It seems likely that international travel could be restricted for some time, so people are planning family camping trips closer to home and embarking on local adventures.

I'm fortunate to have the bush on my doorstep, so, when I'm not working, I can spend days roaming in nature with my family – building bush camps, creating our own nature trails or gardening. In areas experiencing strict restrictions, backyard camping is providing great novelty and fun for families. Our family has a canvas tent permanently set up in our backyard, with a fire pit for campfire cooking. It's also a good spot for mid-winter stargazing and a way for the family to get our nature fix.

Tent Life has grown out of my experiences and growing understanding of the many benefits of camping. This is a guide to every kind of camping, sprinkled with some useful tips and (I hope) inspiration to help you connect with nature and cultivate a sense of freedom.

Now it's up to you to get outdoors and find the magic.

Doron Francis

**For my adventure buddies
Stephanie, Anais, Raffe & Theo.**

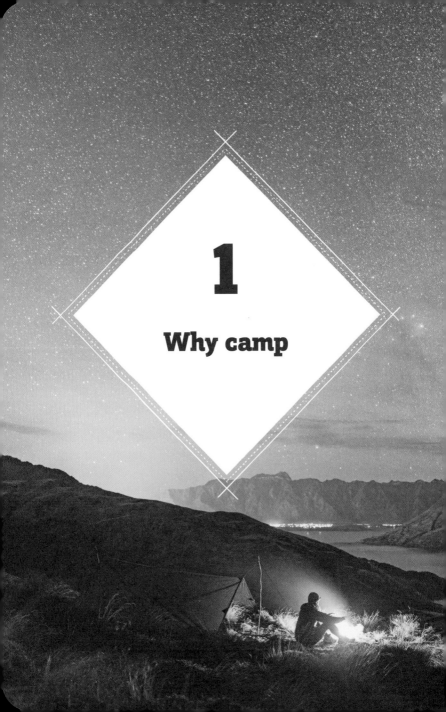

1

Why camp

Wellbeing

Without doubt, the modern world has brought us great material comfort with seemingly endless food options, labour-saving devices, entertainment and inexpensive travel. Unfortunately these developments have not been without cost to both our personal and environmental health.

More than ever before, people are suffering from diseases our ancestors wouldn't recognise – heart disease, obesity, diabetes, anxiety, depression, and many other illnesses that are linked to lifestyle. Alarmingly, there are now ailments such as attention deficit hyperactivity disorder, insomnia and other emotional and physical illnesses that are connected specifically to the widespread adoption of electronic devices and (possibly) social media.

What is clear is that we are collectively suffering from what author Richard Louv calls nature-deficit disorder. We have never before been so connected by technology and yet so disconnected from nature.

Time spent outdoors, particularly for young people, has more than halved in the last 20 years, with one study in the United Kingdom reporting that nearly 50 per cent of parents let the 'fear of strangers' prevent them from allowing their kids to play outside. As Lenore Skenazy points out in her book *Free-range kids*, children are growing up with anxiety, a fear of risk-taking, less ability to evaluate uncertainty, and an inability to build resilience against the hard knocks of reality.

While this paints a bleak picture, the good news is that there are simple and effective remedies that can help alleviate some of these problems, and camping is one of them. There are now many studies linking nature exposure with major benefits in physical and mental health.

A health tonic

Science is now catching up with what campers already know – a digital detox accompanied by time spent in nature has the potential to heal. Numerous studies are saying that nature connectedness is beneficial for general health and, in particular, mood, vitality, cognition and life satisfaction.

Much is being made of nature therapies like the Japanese shinrin-yoku (forest bathing) and mindfulness in nature (*see* p. 217). Studies show that these practices can have a positive impact on our lives and can restore health by repairing our immune system, improving sleep, reducing stress and creating positive effects on our cardiovascular and respiratory function.

My own experience of joining the dots between wellbeing and nature has developed from simple trial and error. I've noticed the effects of long periods spent as a city dweller, and what then happens when I retreat into nature. I gain more focus, a deeper sense of peace and a grateful perspective on life and the world around me. I am now lucky enough to live in a semi-rural area with easy and regular access to hikes in nature. I can attest that getting out for a daily walk, or a more vigorous hike, has made a noticeable positive difference to my own personal state of being (my family all report the same).

Comfort, convenience and choice

You may be wondering why would you want to leave your comfortable life to embark on an outdoor adventure. For better or worse, modernity has given us an overabundance of comfort, convenience and choice. But as Barry Schwartz outlines in *The paradox of choice*, this comes at a price. Not only does the modern lifestyle drain resources and take a heavy toll on our environment, but I also believe it can negatively affect our mindset and attitude towards even the slightest hardship.

When you stop to think about it, we are in an unusual point in history. Never before have so many of us had access to so many (often unhealthy) food options, conveniently delivered to our door. Add to this the infinite entertainment choices available from our ever-present screens and throw in the dopamine hit from social media likes, and it's pretty obvious that the result is an unhealthy recipe for humankind.

In my opinion, one of the most underrated benefits of camping is the opportunity to embrace the challenge of living outdoors. Camping is not an easy holiday, and you can often find yourself questioning why you wanted to set up a tent in the middle of a muddy paddock, with the whole family shouting at each other. Camping reduces choice, convenience and (sometimes) comfort. And this is no bad thing.

There are many rewards. Almost anyone can camp and it's a fun way to develop some basic skills and self-reliance.

There's satisfaction to be had from setting up your camp, building a fire and cooking a meal out in nature. It can help you appreciate what you have (decent plumbing and a hot shower!) and the good things in life.

As our lives become increasingly convenient and comfortable, many of us crave getting back-to-basics and appreciating the simple life. For me, there's no better way to experience these things than camping in the wilderness.

Cost

There are many different ways that you can choose to spend your free time and with the pre-pandemic cost of international travel at an all-time low, people were drawn to 'all-inclusive' deals and a taste of the exotic. But these bargain holidays have hidden costs – the time and stress of getting to the airport and finding parking that doesn't cost a fortune, then the headache of getting through security, followed by a long-haul flight with awful airplane food. The whole experience is energy-draining. More and more – even before the pandemic hit – people have been asking themselves: is it really worth it?

Even a basic calculation of costs will quickly reveal that the holiday you thought was a bargain is really quite expensive when compared with camping. There are no flights to pay for on a camping trip – you usually drive to your destination. Your accommodation costs are low, if not free. The food you eat while camping costs similar to what you would eat at home, and cooking on a gas burner or campfire (even better) costs next to nothing.

Yes, there is some expense in getting the gear together in the first place, and of course fuel for the trip, but the return on investment can be huge. Plus, you can always borrow gear from friends and family while you get your own kit established.

Social camping

Camping solo has its rewards but camping in a group creates great social bonds. It's an active way to share quality time and meaningful experiences with friends and family. There's something special about the shared adventure of camping in a group that encourages connection between new acquaintances and deepens the bonds of existing friendships. I have renewed strong friendships after just a few beverages around a campfire and a couple of days in the bush – it's the quality time and the act of sharing the responsibilities of camp life that brings you together.

It always amazes me how quickly a group of people can start working productively together around a camp – each person taking on particular roles and responsibilities. Now that I have kids and we camp as a family, its noticeable how the kids take on tasks, and how we bond as a unit.

2

Camping lowdown

When to go camping

You may think that the height of summer is the best time to go camping, but each season offers its own unique magic and opportunities. When to go really depends on the conditions in your region and climate zone.

SPRING

In more temperate regions weather can be unpredictable, but one thing's for sure, in spring there's a good chance of rain. On the plus side, after a long winter everything is lush and full of life, with flowers beginning to bloom and grassy meadows appearing. Waterfalls and rivers are in full flow. Campfires will almost certainly be allowed.

If you're planning on visiting arid or desert regions, this can be a spectacular time to camp. Dry regions are warming up quickly and these zones tend to see the most rainfall in spring. Blooming flowers are particularly evocative in deserts. I'll never forget camping trips during wildflower season in the Northern Territory in Australia – the pastel tones of the mulla mulla, curry wattle and the vibrant desert peas against the red earth was a visual feast that truly heightened our hiking experience.

In spring, rivers and watering holes are as full as they'll ever be. Daytime temperatures are usually tolerable and nights are cool. There's generally no fire ban in place, which means that you can have some top-notch camping experiences (think campfire and stargazing time!).

This can still be a good time to head to tropical zones, but towards the end of spring the wet season begins. As the humidity increases, so do seasonal storms and refreshing (for some!) daily downpours.

SUMMER

This is the most popular time to go camping. Most parts of the world have long summer holidays when kids are off school, and families hit the road in search of a break. You can count on the least rainfall but the potential for hot and humid conditions. This is a prime time to explore coastal areas, with beach camping and water-based sports giving relief from the heat. It's also a good time to visit the cooler mountainous regions and river valleys with flowing water on hand to cool off.

Booked out campsites and crowds can be an annoyance at this time of year, so it pays to plan ahead and be creative. In the past I have managed to find small private campsites that are a short drive inland from the busy coast. If the campsite is small enough and you can get enough friends together, try to book the entire site. You can avoid the crowds and the kids can run wild without disturbing any neighbours.

In Australia, flies and mosquitos can be a major hassle. I'll always remember a camping trip in Margaret River, Western Australia with some good friends. We were camping next to an isolated beach on

New Year's Eve with a perfect sunset over the ocean before us. We had great company and a chilled glass of wine – everything was perfectly blissful until we noticed an intense buzzing drone sound behind us. It wasn't long before a huge dark cloud came into view from behind the sand dunes. It turned out to be a swarm of mosquitos (also known as a scourge of mosquitos, for obvious reasons!). Within seconds we were immersed in the swarm and were literally covered head to toe in biting mosquitoes (apparently they can smell humans at a range of 50 metres!). The only thing we could do was evacuate into the sea and escape by following the coastline until they could no longer get a whiff of us.

In summer, the opportunity for a campfire might be limited, and in some regions a complete fire ban will be in place. Australia, Southern Europe and the West Coast of the United States are particularly affected by the potential for wildfire during this period.

In the tropics, heat plus humidity makes this time of year particularly challenging. Arid and desert regions should be avoided.

AUTUMN

Autumn can be the best time to go camping. The weather is generally more settled – not too hot, not too cold, summer winds have died down and, joyously for many, there are less biting insects. In wooded regions, particularly in Europe and North America, deciduous trees are turning red, burnt orange and gold.

It's a fact that kids love rolling around in leaves, and mid- to late autumn is the perfect time for this! In our home state of Victoria, the town of Bright and the surrounding Alpine High Country are particularly majestic at this time of year. Our kids have loved taking full advantage of the fallen leaves from giant oaks, elms, poplars and maples during camping trips to this region.

In autumn, the sun rises a little later and mornings in your tent are cooler (it's a good season to get in some restorative sleep). Chores around camp and hiking adventures are a lot easier in the cooler daytime air. With the exception of Easter in the Southern Hemisphere, campsites are generally quieter and less likely to be booked out. Creating a cosy camp is extremely satisfying at this time of year.

If you're a stargazer (*see* p. 209), many favourite planets and constellations start appearing. Cassiopeia comes into view and Fomalhaut shines brightly, while in the Southern Hemisphere the Emu makes an appearance. It also starts getting darker earlier, so you don't have to stay up too late to get a fantastic view of the stars. For photographers, the light is softer and early morning mists can give extra atmosphere to a landscape shot.

Arid and desert regions are cooling down and this can be a good time to visit as many outback parks begin to open again. However, water can be scarce in arid zones at this time of year, with rivers running low or not at all.

Autumn is heading into the dry season in many tropical regions, so it's a good time to camp in these areas.

WINTER

With the right gear and reasonable weather, winter can be a surprisingly satisfying season to camp in. But be aware that a certain amount of precaution needs to be taken. Good planning and understanding the terrain and weather conditions before you go is important. Keeping dry and warm is a necessity. If you're camping in an alpine region or in the snow, you'll certainly need to invest in a fit-for-purpose shelter, sleeping bag, bedding and clothing (the 'three layer rule' will definitely apply).

Food choice and preparation will need more thought as you'll require extra calories in order to keep warm. Keeping an open fire going for most of the time you spend around camp (breakfast, lunch and dinner) will become a welcome preoccupation.

One of the best reasons for winter camping is that you'll often be the only campers at the campground. What's more, insects, as well as bigger critters like snakes or bears, are nowhere to be seen!

Camping in a gentle snowstorm can be a beautiful experience, creating a serene and peaceful vibe. Combine this with a woodfire stove in your tent (otherwise known as a hot tent, *see* p. 108) and you have the ultimate in hygge – a Danish type of content cosiness – secure from the elements.

Winter is the coolest time to camp in arid or desert regions but be careful as it can drop below zero, with occasional snow and frost on the ground.

Types of camping

Where to camp depends mostly on who you're camping with (kids, solo or friends), your experience and personal preferences. Ask yourself these questions: can you go without a shower or a flush toilet? Are you planning on camping with a vehicle nearby? Will you be hiking and camping?

For me, there's nothing better than a truly 'free' camp with just a swag and a fire, but of course my wife and kids have other ideas! As a family we tend to enjoy camping in national parks which offer a sense of seclusion but also have some bare minimum amenities to keep everyone happy.

The best advice when starting out is to keep it simple. For example, if you're an absolute beginner or camping with kids, you might want to consider setting up camp in your garden as a first step.

GARDEN

If you're a newbie, the easiest way to get to know your gear, and a fun way to introduce kids to camping, is by setting up camp in your garden. (If you live in an apartment then invade a friend or family's garden.) If you have a new tent this will give you a chance to set it up, making sure you have all the necessary parts (and spares) to make your first real camping trip a success.

It's a lazy camp in that you don't need to pack as everything is on hand. There's no eco-guilt or need to carbon offset your trip! It's also a good chance to test run your essentials – bedding, cooking gear and your lighting set-up (*see* p. 31).

As I now have a couple of young kids (two and four at the time of writing), for a large part of the year we have a tent set up in the garden. Kids love having their own camp where they can play. They often act out themes from a real camping trip – pretending to make fires, cook food, dish out chores and shout at each other, just like real life!

FESTIVAL CAMPING

Multi-day music and lifestyle festivals have been gaining popularity for years, and this can be the first experience of camping that kids or young adults have. In fact, my wife and I met while camping at a well-known music festival in Victoria, Australia. From then on, each year we would create festival campsites with our friends, getting more elaborate over time – building giant bamboo geometric domes for a communal area, a shared kitchen area, chill out tents and so on. Things have changed a bit for us since those days with the arrival of kids, but our love of festival camping remains.

Much like camping in your garden, attending a family-friendly festival is another good way to introduce kids to camping and will help you gain confidence for more adventurous camping. Food, toilets and showers are generally on hand, which means you can concentrate on the bare essentials – shelter, bedding and fun around the campsite.

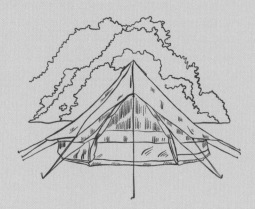

CARAVAN AND CAMPING PARKS

Another way to get a taste for camping without too much planning and commitment is by staying in caravan and camping parks. This type of camping is hugely popular with families as a lot of the larger campgrounds are geared towards activities for kids, thus giving parents peace of mind (and a bit of a breather). I have fond childhood memories of making great friends during week-long park camping trips. I would head off adventuring all day with my new mates until we were called back for dinner.

Caravan parks offer a sense of order and security that many people, particularly families, find attractive. You'll usually be camping on well-manicured soft grass instead of dirt and leaf litter! Unlike nature, trees will be positioned to provide just the right amount of shade, and there'll be electricity and water piped right into your campsite. There are generally other facilities, including shower blocks, a laundry, entertainment options, play equipment and even a swimming pool (or two!).

Often the larger private campgrounds will be packed to the rafters in peak season with families who camp there each year. There's a special social aspect to these campsites, with parents sharing a cool beverage at sundown and kids making new friends. This type of camping should not be discounted, especially for a beginner or family.

PRIVATE CAMPGROUNDS

There's a new and growing phenomenon of smaller campgrounds being set up on private properties. In the United States and Australia, Hipcamp is a website that connects campers with campsites on farmland and rural properties. This is a win-win situation for campers and landowners as often these sites are in beautiful but remote parts of the property on land that is under-utilised. HomeCamper in the United States is also a similar model, and Tentrr, also in the United States, is another that incorporates glamping (*see* below), so you need only turn up with your food and enjoy the view.

GLAMPING

Glamping (a term that is a combination of 'glamorous' and 'camping') describes a more luxurious camping experience. Usually glamping tents are large canvas tents, sometimes with an ensuite, that will already be set up for you. They have hotel-like amenities – a real bed and mattress, bedding, furniture and other decorations – to make the experience ultra-comfortable.

You can often find glamping accommodation near places of beauty, like national parks, so this can be an excellent option to experience walking in nature with a comfortable base to return to. Most glamping sites will provide gear for camp cooking, and often a campfire. So for beginners this can be a less daunting way of getting some of the benefits of camping without the same level of commitment.

It's clearly cheating, but if it means getting the 'never camper' in your life introduced to the concept of sleeping in a tent, then so be it!

NATIONAL PARKS

For me, camping is all about getting away from the crowds and exploring nature. National parks are areas of outstanding beauty, so they're a good choice for starting your love affair with camping and hiking. Designated sites will often need to be reserved, particularly in peak times (try to avoid them). Sites are usually large enough for your car, tent and a cooking/kitchen area. Amenities will often include a toilet, most likely a drop toilet (that sits above a pit and doesn't flush), and potentially access to a shower. If you're lucky there will be a fire pit and wood available.

In national parks you'll usually need to pay entry fees and be aware of the park rules and regulations. Take care not to disturb flora and fauna, and always practice the Leave No Trace camping mantra (see p. 22). Be aware that some parks and campgrounds can get extremely busy at peak times.

BACK-COUNTRY CAMPING

Back-country camping – or bush, primitive, wild or dispersed camping, depending on where you live – is some of the best camping you can experience. It's usually on publicly owned land – national or state forestry, Bureau of Land Management, Landcare, reserve or wildlife trust management areas. The beauty is that often there is often no designated campsite, or if there is, it will be basic.

The rule of thumb is that the harder the site is to get to, the less people it will attract. This means that you can often find complete solitude and experience the wonders of the wilderness without any intrusions.

Accessibility by vehicle is usually more difficult and can be via an unmade or gravel road. Having no designated campsite will also mean no facilities like toilets, fire pits or tables. So remote camping requires more planning.

Some more remote camps will only have access by boat, 4WD or foot. In Australia and parts of the United States and Canada, camping in remote areas is quite common but they are often only accessible

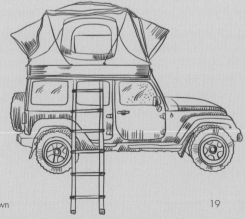

with a 4WD. This type of camping requires certain skills, knowledge and experience to stay safe. Extra communications, GPS and tools are required, and sufficient driving skills and logistical planning comes into play.

Of course, the availability of this type of camping depends on where you live, your vehicle and how long you have for your trip. I suggest building up to back-country camping, as you'll need extra provisions for food, water, fuel, rubbish and waste disposal.

HIKING

Depending on where you live, hiking, backpacking, tramping, bushwalking, rambling and trekking are all different terms for the same thing – essentially, a long walk in the countryside. Set over one to three days, a short multi-day hike is part of the type of camping that is usually done in national parks or designated wilderness areas. Normally hikers will start at one point and hike a circuit, returning to that point after a number of days hiking and camping at night.

Hiking can involve longer stints of walking across wilderness trails and many countries have iconic walks that can take many days, weeks or even months to complete. The Camino de Santiago in Spain, Lycian Way in Turkey, Appalachian Trail in the United States, Overland Track in Australia or the Milford Track in New Zealand are all examples of world-famous walks.

Established end-to-end trail hiking that continues in one direction is known as thru-hiking. This type of walking can require serious planning, with high levels of fitness and specialist gear (*see* p. 158).

Eco credentials

Imagine this. You're walking in a perfect forest, breathing in the fresh air and taking in the atmosphere of your beautiful surrounds, when you stumble upon signs of humanity, often in the form of small trees cut down, a fire pit, broken glass and some beer cans (who are these people?). It's an infuriating sight but fortunately not that common.

There's no doubt that camping can take its toll on the environment but if approached thoughtfully the impact on nature can be minimised (*see* p. 22) and it can also be an eco-friendly alternative to an overseas trip. Unlike a holiday abroad, you're in control of your shelter, the food you consume and how you deal with cooking and waste. These are all opportunities to make conscious decisions about your impact.

More than this, camping has the potential to deepen a pre-existing commitment to taking care of the environment, or introduce a more eco-aware mindset to those who may never have considered their impact before. Even the act of planning your food, water and fuel for a few days inspires a more respectful approach to the resources that we consume.

Leave No Trace: Principles to camp by

If you've ever spent time hoping to visit pristine nature only to find empty beer cans and cigarette butts, you'll know how depressing and ugly it is. As more and more people are visiting wild places, there's a greater urgency for people to take responsibility for their impact on the environment. Luckily most people seem to be waking up and there's a better sense of how we should behave when visiting our precious wilderness.

A fantastic resource to educate yourself and others on how to minimise your impact is produced by the non-profit organisation, Leave No Trace. Their approach is to offer sensible and flexible guidance which aims to cultivate 'an attitude and awareness' of best practices, rather than strict rules and regulations.

Their Australian guide has the following advice:
- plan ahead and prepare
- travel and camp on durable surfaces
- dispose of waste properly
- leave what you find
- minimise campfire impacts
- respect wildlife
- be considerate of your hosts and other visitors

PLAN AHEAD AND PREPARE

Bad planning often means bad results which leads to destruction of the environment. For example, giving no thought to food or human waste disposal.

TRAVEL AND CAMP ON DURABLE SURFACES

Pristine land can be fragile and easy to erode, so stick to worn paths and trails.

DISPOSE OF WASTE PROPERLY

This means all waste, from grey water through to human and food waste. Leave No Trace recommend a 'pack it in, pack it out' approach – don't bury or burn any trash and food scraps even if they are biodegradable. Scatter dishwater and don't be tempted to wash dishes in a stream – the chemicals from detergents can kill fish and other water life. In some environments you may even need to pack out human waste (eww, but necessary!). But where it is allowed, bury all human waste in a cathole 15–20cm (6–8in) deep and 60m (200ft) from water. Where possible and required pack out all hygiene products and used toilet paper. If you cannot pack out your used toilet paper, bury it in a cathole.

LEAVE WHAT YOU FIND

'Take only memories, leave only footprints' is a well-known mantra for outdoor people, and for good reason. Don't tamper with the environment by building structures, leaving toilet trenches unfilled or scarring trees. Don't remove plants, rocks or natural objects that you find.

MINIMISE CAMPFIRE IMPACTS

Campfires can have a huge impact on the environment, and not only when they get out of control. Always use an established fire pit if it's available. Keep fires to a reasonable size and burn all wood down to ashes, ensuring that the fire is completely extinguished. Scatter the ashes after a campfire (making sure there are no embers in the ash!).

RESPECT WILDLIFE

Having been attacked by crazed animals with a taste for barbecue food, I can tell you that keeping food well out of their way is the best approach. Don't ever feed them and, it seems obvious, but don't approach them either. Ensure you never leave waste where animals can get to it (including human waste). Make sure you secure it safely and out of the way.

BE CONSIDERATE OF YOUR HOSTS AND OTHER VISITORS

Look out for your fellow adventurers. Be polite, respectful and helpful to your campsite neighbours and other people you encounter – not just because it's the right thing to do; you never know when you may need a hand. Give way to other hikers on the trail. Keep camp noise to minimum.

3

Preparation

Does it need to be uncomfortable?

My first camping experiences were family trips, with gear mostly borrowed from friends and relatives, and my memories are of uncomfortable (inevitably cold and wet) nights thanks to leaky canvas tents and hopeless bedding – sharing a sleeping bag with cousins and sleeping on a piece of thin foam, if we were lucky! Still, they were always fun and memorable experiences.

But many people have been turned off camping because they've already had an uncomfortable experience, or because they imagine that they will. Often bad planning, disorganisation, inadequate gear and food are the culprits, rather than camping itself.

This is unfortunate as there are many different ways to camp and one bad experience shouldn't end with the conclusion that 'camping is not for me'. If you're organising the trip, you need to be conscious of your 'team'. What might be perfectly acceptable for you in terms of comfort, may not be for your companions.

In my teens and early twenties, I can remember taking various girlfriends on camping trips and some being an absolute disaster. Looking back, it could have been a better experience with some simple upgrades to my gear, in particular to sleeping gear and bedding. A better sleeping pad (or even just a sleeping pad!) or a bit more thought about the food would have helped lighten the experience, especially in rainy conditions.

It's true that a few days in the bush in wet and humid conditions with minimal gear, voracious leeches, freeze-dry food and exhausting hikes is not everyone's cup of tea. But what about a week on a beautiful remote beach in a large tent with a super comfortable bed, excellent food cooked on a gas barbecue and a cold beverage on hand? You could add a solar-powered portable shower, fridge/freezer system and even a TV – does that make it more attractive?

There really is no limit to the amount of gear available to make your camping trip more comfortable, if not downright luxurious. There's no reason to rough it if you don't want to. You can create a camping set-up that fits within your own comfort zone.

Of course, there are limits to what you can physically take with you. And if you're car camping the capacity of your vehicle, choice of gear and budget will determine how comfortable your camp is.

Car camping

Lightweight camping is great, but there's nothing like a camp out in nature with a few home comforts to make it that much more enjoyable. For this reason, I think one of the best ways to start your camping career is by car camping.

One of the many joys of camping with transport – whether that's a 4WD set-up, campervan or a standard car – is that it lets you set up a fully functional and comfortable campsite. It encourages you to stay awhile and tune in to your surroundings. It also allows you to take along items you would never consider on a lightweight adventure: a larger tent, comfortable mattress, cooler, camp kitchen, cast-iron cooking gear, maybe even that camp shower! The only limit is your vehicle's storage capacity. Safety is the priority, of course (*see* p. 85).

With car camping, you can usually drive right to your campsite, unload and set up your camp with everything on hand. This is a great way to camp for families, and means that you have fewer restrictions on weight and size. So you can bring a bigger tent and those toys your kids simply have to have.

Having a vehicle on hand means you can visit surrounding landmarks, parks and walks. You can also drive to the nearest town for supplies (or a cooked meal, if you must!).

What to take

Happily, camping gear has improved immeasurably in terms of quality, availability and price over the years. For many beginners, choosing what gear to take on camping trips can be daunting, with seemingly endless possibilities. Yes, it does seem like a huge investment up-front, but after only a few uses it pays itself off. Plus most gear can be used for other purposes around your home. For example, a lantern for lighting up a garden dinner, a sleeping pad for the kids' play date, a folding saw for pruning in the garden.

Conversely, you'll already own many suitable items for your first camping trip, or you can borrow them from friends. Of course, there's a thriving second-hand market for outdoor gear, too – people are always upgrading or moving. So check online or at your local charity or thrift store where you'll find a lot of good gear at cheap prices.

The more you camp the more you'll want to have a dedicated kit that is packed and ready to go at a moment's notice. But this takes time and expense. Plus you'll need somewhere to store it. This isn't always practical for an inner-city apartment, but it's something to build towards.

Aside from clothing, the essential gear for camping trips consists of a combination of six main elements – shelter, kitchen, bedding, tools, lighting and cleaning. The what, where and how will dictate what you need to take. What are the likely conditions? Where are you planning to camp? And how long for?

Shelter

There's myriad camping shelters available, ranging from ultra-lightweight hammock systems through to elaborate giant tipis made from heavy-duty canvas. The type of camping shelter you choose will be determined by its intended use – the terrain, environment and weather conditions you expect to encounter – and, of course, budget.

Are you camping solo or as a group? Do you need to store equipment in the tent? Are you planning to camp in four seasons? In snow?

For multi-day hikes, bulk and weight will be the main consideration. If you're car camping with a family, space and ease of set-up will be your main priority. If you're planning a semi-permanent set-up on your property, overall comfort and the longevity of the materials that will be exposed to the elements will become much more important.

The single biggest expense in manufacturing a tent is usually the fabric, and the material used has the most influence on your camping experience. Each material has its own advantages and disadvantages so understanding fabrics will help you determine any compromises you'll need to make when choosing a style of tent.

MATERIALS
Cotton canvas

This is the traditional material used for tents that your grandparents would recognise.

Upsides

- Breathable – absorbs some moisture and lets small amounts of air in and out, so there's much less condensation than synthetics (nylon, polyester).

- Fabric coating – advances in technology mean cotton canvas is now much more water, UV and mildew-resistant than it once was.

- Insulation – good thermal qualities mean cotton canvas is cooler in summer and warmer in winter than synthetic tents.

- Less noise – no annoying flapping sound in the wind.

Downsides

- Weight and bulk – cotton canvas tents can be heavy and bulky so they're best suited to car camping.

- Low tear strength – depending on the thickness of the canvas, pure cotton has a relatively low tear strength compared to other fabrics.

- Expense – high quality cotton canvas is expensive.

- Mould – even with a mildew protection treatment, cotton canvas can still be prone to mould.

- Maintenance – canvas needs fairly regular cleaning and reproofing to protect it from damage.

Poly-cotton canvas

Poly-cotton is a derivative of cotton canvas with polyester thread woven into the fabric.

Upsides

- Strength – the polyester makes the canvas stronger than cotton and less likely to tear.
- UV- and mildew-resistant – the polyester gives the canvas improved protection from UV and mould.
- Breathability – canvas will still breathe, so there's less condensation.
- Insulation – poly-cotton is a good insulator against the cold and heat.

Downsides

- Expense – high quality poly-cotton with a good quality coating can be expensive.
- Weight and bulk – although stronger than 100 per cent cotton, poly-cotton tents can still be heavy and bulky.
- Maintenance – while it's more forgiving than cotton canvas, it will need to be reproofed every now and again.

Nylon

Nylon is a good choice for when weight and strength are a major consideration, and it's an ideal material for lightweight hiking.

Upsides

- Strength – nylon can be exceptionally strong – the higher the denier and thread count, the stronger the fabric.
- Lightweight – perfect for ultralight and lightweight camping, with a better strength-to-weight ratio than polyester.

- Water-resistant – usually coated with polyurethane (PU), silicone (aka silnylon), making it waterproof and quick to dry.

- Packs up small – much less bulk than cotton canvas.

- Less maintenance – more resistant to mildew than cotton.

Downsides

- Can lose shape – the fabric can stretch when wet.

- UV damage – susceptible to damage from UV exposure.

- Lacks insulation – not great in the cold and heat.

- Breathability – doesn't breathe and condensation can be a problem, so look for a tent with good ventilation.

- Can tear – look for ripstop nylon for extra strength.

- Cost – good quality nylon tents can be expensive.

Polyester

Possibly the most common tent fabric, polyester is inexpensive, lightweight, fairly strong and a good choice for a festival or large family tent.

Upsides

- Size versus cost – much more affordable when compared to nylon and cotton.

- Low stretch – keeps its shape even when wet.

- Water-resistant – waterproof when coated with the appropriate coating (silicone or PU).

- Weight and bulk – relatively lightweight compared to cotton, and it packs down reasonably small.

Downsides

- Low UV resistance – eventually degrades to the point of being unusable. Being completely synthetic, it's not earth-friendly to dispose of.

- Breathability – doesn't breathe well, so trapping heat and condensation is an issue.

- Low tear strength – compared to similar denier nylons, polyester has a low tear strength. To compensate, manufacturers use thicker fabric, but this adds weight, so it's better suited to car camping.

Dyneema

Formerly known as Cuban fibre, Dyneema Composite Fabric (DCF) is a space-age composite material. Due to its strength and weight, it's a favourite of the ultra-lightweight camping community.

Upsides

- Strength and weight – DCF is the strongest tent fabric for the lowest weight available and has exceptionally high tear strength.

- Water-resistant – doesn't absorb water and is inherently waterproof.

- Keeps its shape – almost no stretch.

- UV resistance – much better UV resistance than nylon, polyester and cotton.

Downsides

- Lacks abrasion resistance – despite being strong, DCF is vulnerable to abrasion.

- Condensation – while not as bad as silnylon, condensation can still be a problem.

- Noise – rustles in the wind.

- Cost – DCF tents are eye-wateringly expensive.

COMMON SHELTERS FOR
CAR CAMPING AND HIKING
Wall tents
4–12 person

Wall tents are large tents
with rigid pole frames of
either steel or aluminium.
Generally, they have a long
ridge pole – and hence
are sometimes known as a
ridge tent – supported by

vertical poles and rafters. Wall tents are usually made from cotton
canvas and can be very solid. They are sometimes freestanding –
they don't require guy ropes, or need to be pegged in.

This classic design is often used by hunters and explorers as a
base camp. It can be large enough to sleep a dozen or more people,
along with a full kitchen and stove set-up. But wall tents are
heavy and take considerable time and effort to set up, so they're
best suited for season camping or long-term camping trips.

Single pole tent
1–8 person

Single pole tents come in a variety of styles – tipi, bell, laavu and
pyramid – and different sizes, materials and features.

Laavu and pyramid tents are usually
made from lightweight technical
materials like silnylon. They're
most commonly used
by bushcraft or solo
hikers who enjoy the
minimalist approach
to camping. Sometimes
these types of tents are

designed for use with a woodfire stove and will incorporate a stove jack or flue exit hole. If you're considering a stove in your tent, *see* p. 108.

Tipi and bell tents are more likely to be made from thicker cotton or poly-cotton canvas and are usually quite large, about 3–6m (10–20ft) in diameter and up to 3.5m (11.5ft) at the apex height. The other main advantage of these tents is that they have minimal parts and are simple to set up.

They are much-loved by the glamping community, but they're also an excellent choice for a base camp or family camping tent as they are spacious (usually 4–8 person), relatively easy to set up, durable and very sturdy in bad weather. Bell tents incorporate a secondary pole at the entrance which gives the tent a unique shape. Canvas bell tents can be heavy and so are best suited to car camping and semi-permanent set-ups.

Cabin tent

2–6 person

This is generally a large family tent that has a rigid frame of either steel or aluminium poles, with canvas walls and a roof that can be made from a variety of materials – often poly-cotton or nylon walls with a polyester fly.

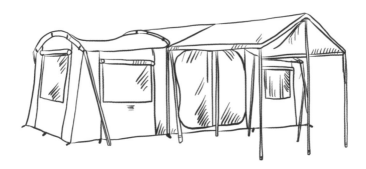

This type of tent can have separate rooms for living and sleeping areas. Families are attracted to cabin tents as they can be more elaborate, with vestibules and awnings to keep kids (and mess) separate from the sleeping area. The walls are usually vertical and the roof fairly high so that there's no need to crouch when moving around the tent.

Look for features like windows and vents, storage and inner tents (a way to divide spaces within a room). You want to have the ability to open doors and windows but still be protected from insects with a mesh screen. There are massive differences in quality for these tents and you usually get what you pay for. Try to ensure that it is relatively easy to pitch as often this type of tent can have complicated designs that lead to stressful set-up situations.

A-frame tent

2–4 person

The classic A-frame scout- or pup-style tent has a triangular shape and a rigid pole frame. They are similar to wall tents but are smaller with fewer parts. Sometimes they will have a horizontal ridge pole linking the vertical poles at each end.

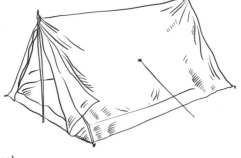

They are generally easy to set up and come in a variety of sizes and a range of materials, from cotton canvas to lightweight versions. Height is usually limited.

Fast or folding frame

2–4 person

This is a variation on the classic frame tent that is becoming increasingly popular. They are essentially steel or extruded aluminium frames that are pre-fitted into the tent shell, usually made from polyester or poly-cotton. The tent unfolds using a

hinge system and, once in place, locks together.

They're extremely easy to set up (some claim 30 seconds!) and it's difficult to lose any parts as they're already incorporated into the system. The drawback is size and weight and, often, expense.

Rooftop tent

2–4 person

Who doesn't love the idea of driving to a beautiful spot with a fantastic view and camping on top of their vehicle? A rooftop tent (RTT) is a fold-out or pop-up hardshell or softshell tent that is fitted onto the roof of a vehicle. They were initially favoured by 4WD enthusiasts and safari-goers who roamed vast distances in outback Australia and Africa, but as prices drop they're becoming more accessible for everyday campers.

Apart from enjoying a good view, one of the many advantages of a rooftop tent is that its quick and easy set-up. Simply unlatch and fold it open, drop the ladder down to the ground and enter your cosy nest. Hey presto – your mattress, bedding, lighting and favourite book will already be in place. There are no poles to put together or pegs to drive into the ground – bliss!

As you don't need to inflate the mattress, it's generally more comfortable than a standard camping mattress. Softshell rooftop tents are usually constructed with waterproofed polyester or cotton-poly canvas (preferred) and a polyester fly. Hardshell rooftop tents are aesthetically neater, easy to secure, more aerodynamic and slightly easier to set up, but are usually more expensive. Other features to look for are plenty of storage space, interior lighting, mesh-screen windows, ventilation, and a useful annex tent that connects to the base of the platform.

Being elevated off the ground has many other advantages – it's easier to catch a night-time breeze and much cooler than camping on the hot ground. There's no need to worry about the local wildlife and harmful critters at ground level and you don't need to find a perfectly flat campsite, so camping on uneven or rocky surfaces is easy.

One of the most underrated benefits of a rooftop tent, particularly in Australia, is that there's much less dirt and dust to deal with, so less time is spent trying to keep your sleeping quarters clean and orderly. The drawbacks are size and weight. Naturally you'll need a rooftop tent that can fit your needs, and two adults and three kids seems to be the limit for the larger sizes. Remember that the tent and bedding will take up a lot of real estate on your roof, which means less room for your cargo boxes and other camping gear.

Before buying, check your vehicle's load ratings (*see* p. 84). While you can mount a rooftop tent on a standard sedan, I recommend an SUV or 4WD (or camper trailer) with enough space to mount the appropriate sized

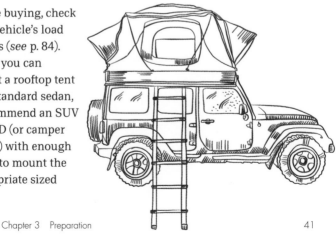

tent. Rooftop tents need to be clamped to the appropriate roof rack system that can handle the extra weight, and getting the tent on and off your roof can require an extra pair of hands.

Finally, rooftop tents can be expensive, so weigh up how much use you'll get from it before purchasing.

Lightweight camping and hiking tents
1–3 person

These are generally smaller tents made from synthetic materials, ranging from ultralight technical fabrics like dynema, through to various nylons, polyesters and other derivatives. Fabrics are the main consideration for this type of tent and there's always a trade-off between performance, size and weight (and cost!).

Lightweight camping tents will usually have flexible pole sections made of fibreglass or aluminium alloy (the best!) that are colour-coded and lock into each other to create a long pole that forms part of the tent frame. Because of the flexible poles, lightweight tents can be made into various shapes – geodesic, dome, tunnel, ridge or pyramid – and each shape has its own inherent advantages. The pole sections are usually connected by an internal elastic cord running the entire length of the pole.

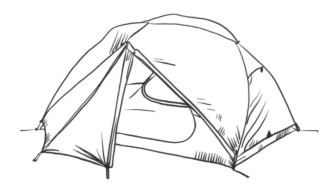

As with just about any product, lightweight tents can range from ludicrously cheap (avoid) to crazy expensive, depending on the materials and other features. Look for well-known brands and check how the tents are constructed. For example, sewn reinforced seams that are sealed (taped) and other reinforcement in areas of tension are an indicator of quality. Generally, they have a separate fly that protects the tent.

Look for the waterproof rating and other features, like mesh doors and vents, tie-down points, pockets and pouches and extra ventilation. YKK is a trusted zip brand that most good tent manufacturers use. Check out how easy it is to pack away and what compression strapping it comes with. A good tent will come with a repair kit.

Swag

1–2 person

The swag is an iconic Australian camping shelter, named after the swagman, an itinerant worker who travelled the country working seasonal jobs  during the 19th century. The swagman slept rough under his swag which was made up of woollen blankets with a canvas cover, much like a cowboy bedroll.

Swags have since developed and are now fully enclosed shelters, with large doors for easy entry and exit, and a mesh inner door that allows you to sleep under the stars but protects you from Australia's many biting and stinging critters. The real beauty of a swag is that you can add a sleeping pad and sleeping bag, so all you need to do is roll it out and you're ready to sleep.

Swags are almost always made from heavy-duty cotton or poly-cotton canvas with a waterproof (sometimes PVC) floor which helps protect against the dusty and extreme environments found in Australia. Swags come in singles or doubles and are usually freestanding shelters. The fancier ones have a pitch system that is more like a small tent. But watch out, once rolled up with all your bedding they're big and heavy beasts.

Hammock and tarp system

1 person

Hammock camping is a good alternative to a tent and they're becoming increasingly popular among the ultralight hiking and bushcraft community. Hammocks are suspended from two anchor points, usually trees. Webbing straps are looped around the tree and have connection points that attach to the hammock with climbing carabiners.

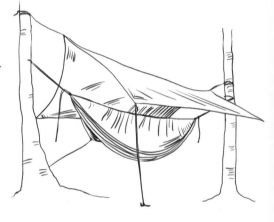

Enthusiasts enjoy the comfort of a hammock and, as the camper is suspended off the ground, there's also less concern about critters or flooded terrain. If rain is likely, a tarp can be suspended above the hammock. There are specialist insulated sleeping pads and under quilts that work well in a hammock set-up, improving comfort and warmth. A good quality hammock will usually be made from high denier ripstop nylon.

Sleeping in a hammock can take some trial and error to get used to, so it's worth trying different sleeping styles until you find one that works for you. Depending on where you live or plan to camp, a decent bug net will probably be an essential part of your set-up.

Bivvy

1 person

Similar to an Australian swag but usually much lighter in weight, the bivvy is another option for sleeping outdoors without a tent. A bivvy is essentially a waterproof cover for your sleeping bag. It ranges from ultra-lightweight (less than 500g/20oz) high-tech fabric to heavier duty ripstop nylon.

Unlike a swag, a bivvy doesn't have a sleeping pad incorporated into the design. Usually the head is a hooded section that may or may not have mosquito netting protection for the face. With cold climate and snow camping, bivvys are often used inside a tent for extra protection from the elements.

BEDDING

Bedding is one of the most important items for camping success. A great sleeping set-up will make the biggest difference in terms of comfort and wellbeing, and therefore your mental outlook and enjoyment of camping. It's surprising that people will put up with an uncomfortable night's sleep because they either don't know that camp bedding – or 'sleep systems' in modern marketing speak – have improved, or they can't justify spending the extra money on good gear. When planning your camping kit I recommend that you don't skimp and make bedding a priority. You need to be warm and dry with the right support.

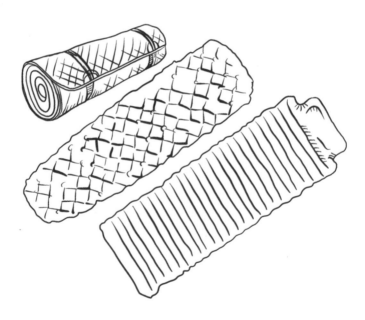

Sleeping pads

As with anything that can be manufactured, there's a huge range of brands and products out there in various styles and materials. But before examining them it's worth understanding the manufacturers' ratings for warmth, which is measured as an R-value. This is simply a way for comparing the thermal resistance and, therefore, insulation properties of a sleeping pad. The higher the R-value the more insulation your pad will have. So as a general rule, the higher the rating the thicker and heavier the pad will be. For example, high R-values are usually associated with pads suitable for car camping rather than hiking.

Sleeping pad R-values range from 1 to more than 10. For cold weather camping it's advisable to look for pads rated 6+. Obviously a good sleeping bag can make up for a low R-value pad and vice versa.

There's always a trade-off between comfort, weight and bulk, which becomes much more important when you're hiking (there are endless threads on hiking forums about this). But it's still a consideration when car camping as there are always limitations with what you can fit in, or on, a vehicle.

Let's look at the main categories of sleeping pads.

Inflatable air pads

Inflatable air pads have come a long way in recent times. Improvements in materials and insulation mean that they can be surprisingly comfortable. Typically inflated using either a pump or breath, air pads can have partitions and internal chambers that are shaped to the contours of the human body. Air is then dispersed consistently throughout the pad, resulting in a more comfortable sleep. Favoured by hiking enthusiasts, air pads have much less bulk when compared to similar weight foam or self-inflating pads.

The drawback with an air pad is that if the outside air is cold then the air in your pad will also be cold, and so you'll be cold too (I have found this out the hard way!). Often manufacturers get around this by using duck down or synthetic fibre inside the air chambers. This is where the R-value comes in, as this will show how good the insulation technology used by the manufacturer is – something you should look for when camping in the colder seasons.

Other drawbacks of inflatable pads are that they can be punctured and are tricky to fix out in the field, and they're noisy when you move around in your sleep – it's good to test this instore.

Self-inflating pads

Self-inflating pads are usually a combination of a polyester or nylon outer layer with an interior made from open-cell foam that can be inflated with air via a valve. Once the valve is open, air is automatically drawn in and the foam expands. Inflation can be finished with a hand pump or breath.

Self-inflating pads come in a variety of weights, and R-values are usually very comfortable and reasonably compact when compared to closed-cell foam. Depending on the materials used, they can be much more durable than blow-up air pads, and if you do get a puncture they're fairly easy to repair. In my experience an 8cm (3in) self-inflating pad is the ultimate in camping comfort and worth finding some room for in your vehicle. Look for a pad with a durable waterproof outer and high-quality quick-inflating valves.

Besides potential bulk and weight, the biggest drawback with self-inflating pads can be expense. A high-quality thick mattress can cost a small fortune!

Foam pads

Foam pads are made using closed-cell foam (CCF) which is essentially dense foam cells formed with high-pressure gas that are sealed off from outside air. CCF requires no inflation and is much firmer and rigid than open-cell foam, offering fairly good back support. The foam is UV stable and doesn't absorb water, so it's a good choice for sleeping outdoors.

Favoured by bushcraft and lightweight campers, CCF pads are simple, durable and inexpensive – a good compromise between weight, warmth and cost. As they're stronger than their self-inflating counterparts and not prone to punctures, they're much less likely to let you down in the field. A good foam pad will have an accordion-like design (Z shaped) which folds together with one softer textured side (much like an egg carton) and the other denser side for durability.

On the downside, CCF are not as comfortable as the same weight self-inflating pad and, despite being lightweight, bulkiness is an issue.

Sleeping bags and bedding

Depending on whether you're car camping or backpacking, there are different sizes, weights and styles of sleeping bags available. The most important feature is going to be size and warmth. Most decent brands will make bags in different lengths, so make sure you have plenty of room for your whole body and head to be covered. The temperature rating is a good guide to what you'll need. As the name suggests, a three-season bag is perfect for most of the year.

Sleeping bags are generally a nylon or polyester shell with a durable water repellent (DWR) coating which prevents moisture from being absorbed. The premium technical fabric dryloft – a version of Gore-Tex – is another popular shell fabric favoured by cold-weather campers because of its water-resistant and breathable qualities.

Sleeping bags are stuffed with either synthetic or down insulation. Synthetic is inexpensive, still insulates when wet and dries easily. Down insulation is lightweight and warm in dry, cold weather and compresses well – it's still the preferred choice of insulation for snow campers. Look for a down that's certified RDS (Responsible Down Standard) or Global TDS (Global Traceable Down Standard).

Bags come in various shapes, with rectangular being the most popular for general camping. The 'mummy' shape is preferred by hikers as it has a hood and a better warmth-to-weight ratio. There are also double bags made for two.

KITCHEN

Being able to cook a hot meal and drink a warming beverage is a must for any camping set-up. You can get by with a basic kitchen kit on a lightweight hike, but if you're camping for multiple days and using a vehicle, and weight is not an issue, it makes sense to have a decent camp kitchen so that you can cook from scratch (*see* p. 140). I have never regretted the extra effort and space it takes to have a proper kitchen set-up.

Here's a basic outline of some of the essentials for an enjoyable camping trip.

Camp stove

Even if you plan to cook on a campfire, it's wise to bring a camp stove as backup for when you need to cook something quickly and easily. Also, there will be times with bad weather or lack of fuel when it'll be difficult to make a fire.

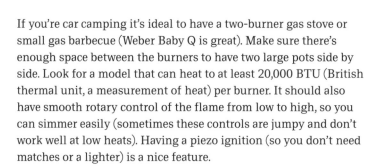

If you're car camping it's ideal to have a two-burner gas stove or small gas barbecue (Weber Baby Q is great). Make sure there's enough space between the burners to have two large pots side by side. Look for a model that can heat to at least 20,000 BTU (British thermal unit, a measurement of heat) per burner. It should also have smooth rotary control of the flame from low to high, so you can simmer easily (sometimes these controls are jumpy and don't work well at low heats). Having a piezo ignition (so you don't need matches or a lighter) is a nice feature.

Your stove should have protective wind barriers that attach to the sides and back. For car camping and long stays, you'll want a stove that can be used with standard LPG gas bottles – 4kgs (8.8lbs) is a good size and will last a couple of weeks at least.

Coolers

Technology for coolers, eskies, ice chests and battery-powered fridges has come a long way. There's a big difference in performance (and price) between a thin, plastic cooler from your local megamart and the latest insulated rotomoulded cooler.

A high-end cooler can keep ice for days at a time, even in hot temperatures. The general rule of thumb is the bigger the better, but remember that they can get heavy when packed with ice and food. I prefer to take two coolers. A soft one for cold beverages and another hard cooler exclusively for food so that the lid isn't opened as much.

Use high-quality pre-frozen ice packs (bricks) either alongside or as an alternative to ice. They'll stay cold a lot longer and there won't be meltwater to deal with. A 35–45L (9–12gal) cooler is a good size for a two- to five-day trip, especially if you have access to more ice for top-ups.

Having a dual battery fitted to your vehicle is like magic for campers! It means that while your engine runs and charges the main battery, you can also charge a separate battery that can be used to power other 12V equipment – like fridges, fans, lights and other gear – without the risk of running down your main battery. Most 4WDs and some SUVs will already have dual batteries or will have the provision for a battery to be added. So, if you have the storage capacity in your vehicle, a camping fridge is an excellent addition as you won't need to worry about sourcing ice. Battery-powered fridges are bulky and heavy but will no doubt be a welcome addition to your kit.

Water containers

Whatever you do, you're going to need to bring some sort of large container of fresh drinking water. Of course you can easily buy disposable plastic bottles from a supermarket, but that's a great waste.

Reusable water containers are available but they're generally rigid plastic tanks or jerry cans that take up a lot of space. Plastic also degrades in sunlight and I hate to think what happens to those chemicals after a short while camping. The water always seems to have that plastic flavour!

I prefer to take water bladders. They range in size from 1L (1qt) up to 200L (53gal)! The advantage is that they aren't rigid like jerry cans and so are more flexible to pack in your vehicle, and to store at home when not in use. Good bladders are suitable for drinking water, are double-walled and are enclosed in a canvas outer bag.

The bladders I use lay across the rear-seat footwell and have a standard inlet/outlet hose and tap. Sometimes bladders have grommets and straps so that you can attach them to your vehicle, or tie them to a tree to use as a makeshift shower.

What size bladder to take depends on what you'll be using it for. With drinking, cooking, cleaning and some basic personal hygiene, 5–10L (1.5–2.5gal) of water per person per day should be plenty. Take more than you need and make sure you fill up at every opportunity.

Take a water filter, water purification tablets or a SteriPEN which treats water with UV light.

Cooking gear

What type of cookware you take camping will most likely be determined by the type of camping you're doing. Typically when camping with a vehicle, weight won't be a major consideration. But on a multi-day thru-hiking trip it wouldn't make sense to take a cast-iron cooking set.

Much like at home, you'll need equipment to prepare, cook and serve your food. Depending on your circumstances (if you're hiking rather than car camping, for example) the methods of cooking your food will change.

Below is an outline of some gear I would consider the most essential for a decent camp kitchen.

Dutch ovens

This could be the only camp cooking vessel you need for a car camping trip and is definitely my go-to for camp cooking. A Dutch oven is a large cooking pot with a bail wire handle which consists of a section of wire with a loop each end that attaches to opposing sides  of the oven lip, like a bucket handle. The oven will have a tight-fitting lid which is usually slightly concave with a raised edge so that hot coals can be placed on top of the oven without falling off. Often Dutch ovens will have small legs underneath so they can be elevated above coals beneath. With coals on top and below you have an oven that radiates heat evenly – perfect for all types of baking, braising and roasting.

Dutch ovens are usually made from cast-iron or carbon steel and can be used as a frying pan, or for boiling water for a brew. Because of the bail handle, it's also handy for transporting water around camp.

Cooking pots

If you're camping without a Dutch oven you'll want some sort of cooking pot. Again, the size and material of the pot will be determined by the type of camping and how many people you're cooking for.

Car camping families should take at least two or three pots that are stackable and fit inside each other – 16, 18 and 20cm (6, 7 and 8in) are good sizes. Look for a set that comes with clip-on handles so you can pack the pots easily. Also look for pots that are suitable for oven cooking – these will survive the extreme heat from a campfire.

For solo adventurers a 1L (1qt) pot would work. For two or more campers, you'll want a bigger 2L (2qt) pot or, even better, two different sized pots that nest into each other.

On a lightweight hiking trip, a good pot will usually be the only cooking vessel you take and it will be used for single-pot cooking. Much like a Dutch oven, try to find a pot with a lid and a bail wire handle so that you can easily retrieve the pot from an open fire, or hang it from a tripod over the fire. Known as a billy in Australia and New Zealand, this type of pot is one of the most versatile pieces of cooking equipment – perfect for boiling water and cooking stews and soups.

Most camping pots are made with stainless steel or aluminium (ideally hard anodised). If you're aiming to reduce weight, go for titanium.

Storm kettle

Of course you can use a small pot for boiling water but a kettle is more efficient. An excellent choice is a storm kettle (also called a volcano or hurricane kettle), which is an old heritage design that is ideal for camping, fishing and hiking.

Storm kettles don't require gas – a little foraged fuel (some twigs and a little paper) will bring water to the boil in no time. These kettles are great fun for kids who can build a little fire to get them going. They are also an excellent emergency device and should find a place in just about any camping kit.

Skillet

A skillet is a shallow frying pan and is almost certainly essential for your kitchen kit. Aside from a pot, it's probably the most used cooking gear on any camping adventure. Skillets come in all sorts of sizes

and weights depending on the material they're made from – if you have to pick one, 25cm (10in) is a good versatile size.

Some skillets have raised sides which are really handy and great for poaching eggs or quickly boiling water. It's recommended to have lids for skillets and pots so they'll heat quickly and then retain heat, making them more efficient. If not, you can always use the base of another pot or pan for a lid!

Toasted sandwich maker and camp toaster

An absolute favourite while camping is a hot sandwich maker, used just about any time of the day for making jaffles (as civilised folk call them) or (if you must) toasties. Whatever your choice of name, stuffed with your favourite ingredients (plus cheese!), you can't go wrong. Kids love them, and rightly so!

A mesh camping toaster is arguably another essential. They're super easy to use – just put your bread between the mesh wire and hold it over the fire or your gas-stove flame. Not too close though.

Utensils

You'll want to bring cutlery – a knife, fork and spoon for each person, and a few spares. If you're conscious of weight and are travelling solo, a spork – a hybrid of the fork and spoon – is ideal. Again, if weight is a concern and money is no object, titanium is fantastic. If not, opt for stainless steel or bamboo. Ideally, avoid single-use plastics which are damaging to the environment.

Also pack a spatula, whisk and serving spoons. It might sound like overkill but a microplane (grater!) gets used a lot – grating lemon zest, truffle, garlic, cheese or chocolate. I recommend having a dedicated storage box, pouch or roll for your utensil kit.

Water bottles

A decent stainless steel water bottle is essential. Don't waste your time with plastic. Aim for about 1L (1qt), either single-walled or the fancier double-walled (vacuum insulated) that will keep hot water hot and cold water cool for longer.

Cups and plates

I'll let you in on a secret – campfire hot chocolate tastes better in a classic enamel mug! Stainless steel is also a good bet but if you're willing to splurge on a titanium double-walled cup it's durable, lightweight, and the vacuum wall keeps your hot chocolate or coffee hot without the cup scalding you. Otherwise there's a plethora of insulated mugs available that will keep your hot beverages hot and your cold, cold.

Plates and bowls made from enamel, stainless steel or bamboo (or other sustainable materials) are recommended. Look for sets of plates and bowls that nest nicely into each other.

Kitchen knives

Aside from a fixed blade and a pocket knife (see p. 67), you'll want some general kitchen knives. For your first few camping trips you may choose to take a couple of knives from your kitchen at home, but a dedicated set of knives that are rugged enough for outdoor use is recommended.

A set of carbon steel knives (stainless steel, if you have to) with gripped polypropylene handles that are aimed at butchers, hunters and fishing enthusiasts is a great idea as they can take a battering and are relatively inexpensive. At the very least, you want a couple of all-purpose chef's knives, a paring knife and a diamond sharpening stone or steel. If you plan on fishing while camping you'll need to bring scaling and filleting knives.

Ideally, your knives will have individual sheaths, or be safely wrapped into a canvas utensil roll, to avoid accidents and dulling the blades.

Chopping board

I recommend bringing a couple of chopping boards, ideally the folding variety. Bamboo is a good choice as it's lightweight and inexpensive.

Barbecue utensils

For barbecuing you'll need prongs, tongs and spatulas that are as long as possible with heat-resistant handles. I always take some long stainless-steel skewers with wooden handles to chargrill meat and veggies. They're inexpensive and are easily available online.

Other kitchen bits

A peeler, can opener and grater will definitely be missed if you don't pack them. Don't forget your bottle opener either. Foil, kitchen towel and plastic cling wrap (or better for the environment, beeswax wrap) will come in handy.

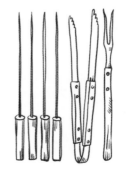

Coffee makers

Thankfully, coffee and coffee makers aimed at campers have come a long way since a spoon full of Nescafé and some long-life milk. Portable grinders, pour-over coffee makers, espresso pumps, and coffee presses are now on hand to ensure you're delivered the right dose for your morning coffee, exactly how you like it.

It's nice to have a dedicated pouch (I use an old canvas Dopp kit) with all your coffee gear in one place. You'll often be up at the crack of dawn and this will be the first task at hand. I'm a big fan of AeroPress or Wacaco Minipresso, although they may well be outdated by the next-big-thing as this book goes to press.

Kitchenware materials

Certain types of cookware are better suited to some materials than others. Most likely your kit will end up consisting of a mix of cookware made from various materials that work best for you.

CAST-IRON

Cast-iron is *the* iconic camping cookware material. It's remarkably hardwearing, taking almost any punishment you can give it, and will outlive most of us. It's loved by chefs because it concentrates the heat and retains it for a long time. It's the perfect cookware for the extremes of campfire cooking. A roast, simple stew or freshly baked bread made with a cast-iron Dutch oven is a camping wonder that will earn you saintly status.

The secret of cooking with cast-iron is keeping it well-seasoned. Seasoning is simply adding a natural non-stick layer to the pan. This is made by coating the pan with a small amount of oil – preferably 100 per cent vegetable oil applied by a non-aerosol sprayer – and getting it red hot (above 180°C or 350°F), either in your home oven or in the hottest part of your campfire. One of the biggest disadvantages of cast-iron is the weight – it's heavy. But for a car camping trip where you're staying a few days, it's well worth it.

ENAMEL

Enamel cookware is part of any classic camping kit. Enamel is a coating that is a bit like glass and is applied to steel as a protective layer. Enamel mugs and plates are highly prized among campers as they're relatively lightweight, durable and easy to clean. Another attraction of enamelware is that it ages gracefully and develops character with time – every dent tells a story of your adventures! Like most things, all enamel is not created equal. Look for enamelware made the traditional way – it's generally weightier and built to withstand all sorts of rigours.

CARBON STEEL

Sometimes known as spun steel, carbon steel is much lighter than an equivalent sized cast-iron pan. It's a great choice for camp cookware – it has similar properties to cast-iron, in that it can handle extreme heat and cooks fairly evenly, but it heats up and cools down more quickly. Carbon steel is more sensitive to heat changes so it has the edge for technical cooking. Unlike cast-iron, there's no risk of it breaking from thermal shock. Carbon steel is also easily seasoned and has a natural non-stick layer which is non-toxic and much tougher than artificial non-stick coatings

STAINLESS STEEL

Weighing in somewhere in between carbon steel and aluminium is the good all-rounder of stainless steel. It's often favoured because it's inexpensive, robust and scratch-resistant, so it's fairly easy to clean. Unfortunately, stainless steel is not the best heat conductor and cooks unevenly, which can result in heat spots that burn food.

Stainless steel is best used with a propane gas burner set-up where you have better control over heat and can fry low and slow. Stainless steel is suited for general cooking pots, mixing bowls, water bottles, cups and utensils. Look for 304-grade stainless steel that has been electro-polished as it's easier to clean and resists corrosion better.

ALUMINIUM AND HARD-ANODISED ALUMINIUM

Aluminium is a lightweight and durable metal that has excellent conductivity and so is ultra-efficient to cook with. It's inexpensive to produce and doesn't corrode. There's the possibility that aluminium will leach and this has been associated with Alzheimer's, so I recommend using hard-anodised aluminium. This has the weight advantages of aluminium but is much stronger.

TITANIUM

Beloved by ultralight hikers everywhere, titanium is the strongest and lightest camp kitchenware material you'll find. Although an excellent choice for cups, plates and utensils, when used for cooking it performs poorly. It heats quickly but disperses energy unevenly and creates hotspots next to the heat source. Titanium pots are mostly used by ultralight hikers to boil water for freeze-dried packet meals. Another drawback of titanium is the expense.

OTHER MATERIALS

For utensils, plates, cups and straws, bamboo and stainless steel are good alternatives to plastic. Silicone is a great non-toxic and flexible material for kids' plates.

LIGHTING

Lighting technology has come a long way since the days of clunky and heavy torches (flashlights) stuffed full of D-size batteries. Advances in LED technology and lithium batteries mean that you can easily find a compact and powerful torch (flashlight) that is less than 10cm (3.9in) long, puts out over 1000 lumens (a car headlight is about 700 lumens!) and weighs less than 150gm (5.3oz). While this is probably overkill and annoying for fellow campers, you can find a happy medium between weight and performance.

Ideally, take more lighting than you need. Preferably, a large handheld torch (flashlight) and a headlamp, plus another spare, along with the necessary batteries.

I also recommend taking a couple of lanterns that have wire handles and can be hung. One that uses rechargeable batteries and another that uses kerosene are a good idea. Storm lanterns are a great choice. I recommend Feuerhand, a German brand that has been manufacturing storm lanterns for over 100 years. They're inexpensive, durable, simple and rarely fail.

Batteries are a necessary evil when camping, which is why it's better to either use products that can run off your car battery, a portable power supply (see p. 73) or rechargeable batteries. Other choices include wind-up torches (flashlights) – very good in emergencies – and solar-powered lights.

For lighting up large areas around camp, like the toilet area, invest in LED strips or bars that will run off battery, 12V or solar. Some can be powered from a cigarette lighter plug. These are low cost, don't require much energy and can be fixed to almost any surface. Some will have features like a remote control (once you have this you'll use it all the time!), dimmer switch, or various lighting modes.

A flood light is a powerful and useful light that lights up the whole campsite. It's recommended for a 4WD camping set-up for safety reasons (or for when you lose your bottle opener!), especially if you're remote camping and arriving to set up camp at night.

CAMP FURNITURE

Sitting on the cold ground is uncomfortable and not conducive to a good time, so a camp chair is an absolute essential for a car camping trip. On a hiking trip some sort of back support is also welcome, especially if you're walking and camping night after night.

Chairs range from lightweight tripod stools to fancy (and expensive) designs with various extras, like cup holders, extra padding and insulation, and even footrests. While a giant moon-shaped camp chair might be wildly comfortable, they can be very bulky and heavy.

When considering weight and comfort, hard-anodised aluminium foldaway frames are the best – they pack down to a package the size of a 2L (2qt) water bottle. Consider how much room you have to pack your gear and how much comfort you really need in order to have a pleasant stay. Make sure the kids have their own little camp chair.

Most official campsites will have a table or shared tables but in remote areas this will not be the case, so invest in a small foldaway table that you can use for kitchen duties and keeping plates of food off the ground. The roll-top designs are useful as they can be easily stored.

TOOLS AND EQUIPMENT

For any serious or semi-serious camping you're going to want to invest in some basic tools for various duties around camp and for use in emergency scenarios.

Multitool

A good multitool is a must. Buy one that has a sheath that can be attached either to your belt or to a lanyard. It's amazing how many times you'll be reaching for it around camp. A classic Swiss Army knife is great to have around (the corkscrew was in constant use back in the day), however these have been replaced somewhat by Leatherman-style tools.

Needle-nosed pliers, scissors, wire cutters, scraping and sawing tools will be used a lot around camp. Having a mini screwdriver on hand is very useful too. The big brands are probably still the best in terms of price, build and features.

Knives

A good knife is an essential camp tool and will be used for many jobs, like cutting rope, emergency repairs, clearing brush, processing firewood or just prepping dinner! While any style of durable knife that is built for outdoor use will come in handy, a classic fixed-blade, full-tang knife is hard to beat. Any outdoorsy person will tell you that it's possibly the only tool you'll need in a survival situation.

'Fixed blade' simply means a knife that is fixed into position, i.e. not the folding variety, and 'full tang' is a blade that extends the full length of the knife from the tip to the end of the knife handle. This makes the knife an extremely strong tool which allows you to use it with a forceful action, providing plenty of leverage.

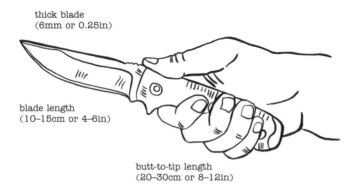

thick blade
(6mm or 0.25in)

blade length
(10–15cm or 4–6in)

butt-to-tip length
(20–30cm or 8–12in)

A good camping knife will have a fairly thick blade (6mm or 0.25in, or more) and weigh up to 300gms (10oz). A good size is between 20–30cm (8–12in) long from the butt (bottom of the handle) to tip, with a 10–15cm (4–6in) blade.

Blade materials

Perhaps the biggest debate among knife aficionados is which blade material is best. As with just about anything, the answer is 'it depends'. Here are some things to consider.

Stainless steel is known for its strength and durability but it's not as sharp as carbon steel. Stainless steel is low maintenance because it's highly resistant to moisture and so doesn't tend to rust or corrode like carbon steel. At the premium end, Japanese and Swedish steel is very popular. Carbon steel is easier to sharpen and stays sharp longer than stainless steel. High carbon steel is very hard, which makes it more resistant to abrasions, but also means the blade is rigid and brittle, so it can crack rather than bend when under stress. There's more potential for corrosion with carbon steel and so more maintenance is required.

When not in use knives should be safely stored in a protective sheath at all times.

Saws

Though it's always tempting to grab an axe, the second most useful tool in your camping armoury will be a saw. It's a much safer tool for felling a small standing tree, or removing a limb and processing it into smaller pieces, than an axe or hatchet.

There are many saws that are suitable for camping and can easily be carried in a backpack. The most popular styles are a folding saw (that folds into a protective sheath), bow saw (a fixed D-shaped frame that is efficient for big jobs) and a pocket saw (a manual chainsaw aimed at campers and hikers that is surprisingly effective at cutting through logs).

Just like knives, saws need to be sheathed at all times when not in use. It's a good idea to use safety gloves and goggles when sawing.

Axes

As one of the oldest human technologies, an axe is a simple but powerful tool that consists of a metal axe head which is sharpened to a cutting edge (known as a blade or bit) and handle (or haft) that is traditionally made of wood.

Axes come in a variety of sizes, weights and head patterns (the shape of the head). You should consider your axe's end-use before you buy one (or two!). Axe blades are usually made from high carbon or stainless steel, with either a wood (hickory or ash are traditional) or synthetic handle. Much like a knife, there are large variations in quality, function and price, with the material used having similar trade-offs in durability, ease of sharpening and resistance to corrosion.

Smaller axes, like a hachet, are most useful for camping. The hatchet is a single-handed axe that is small enough to fit in your backpack on a hike. The larger forest axe is a good compromise between the large felling axe and the smaller hatchet. It's favoured by the bushcraft community because the extra length of the handle provides more leverage and chopping power than a hatchet.

Although swinging an axe and chopping wood is fun and a good workout, using an axe shouldn't be taken lightly as it can cause serious injury if misused (*see* p. 120 for instructions on proper use). Just like your knife, always keep an axe in a secure sheath when not in use.

Shovel or trowel

It's surprising how often you'll use a shovel or trowel around camp – levelling ground before pitching a tent, digging trenches if there's a storm or digging a camp latrine. A shovel is also a handy tool for digging a fire pit or moving hot coals around a campfire. You may need to dig your car out of sand or a bog. If weight and bulk are an issue, get a folding shovel.

Mallet

If you're doing any sort of camping with a large tent on hard surfaces, you'll need a tool with a heavy head to drive in large pegs. While a hammer will do (and a rock will work at a pinch), a mallet with a metal head is a better tool for the job.

First aid and emergency

A decent outdoor first-aid kit is a non-negotiable essential for any camping or hiking trip. They're affordable and you'll never regret having one around. If you have a car, you really should have one that lives in the vehicle anyway.

Unless you're a professional, a pre-made kit is the way to go as you won't overlook key items. At most outdoor stores you'll find first-aid kits that come pre-packed in durable canvas. In some countries it might be wise to have a snake-bite kit.

A good kit should include:

- [ ] bandages – compression, triangular, elastic gauze
- [ ] heavy-duty plasters/bandaids, wound pads and other dressings (hydrogel spray like Burnaid)
- [ ] blister packs
- [ ] antiseptic/alcohol wipes
- [ ] saline solution
- [ ] Leukofix tape
- [ ] antibacterial ointments
- [ ] zinc oxide ointment (relief for chafed skin)
- [ ] antihistamines
- [ ] painkillers – ibuprofen (like Advil, Nurofen) for muscle pain, paracetamol or acetaminophen for general use, Voltaren for inflammation
- [ ] scissors
- [ ] tweezers (aka tick remover!)
- [ ] safety pins
- [ ] hand sanitiser
- [ ] rehydration powders
- [ ] splint
- [ ] Imodium tablets
- [ ] instant ice pack
- [ ] deep heat
- [ ] emergency blanket.

It's good to find out beforehand if a member of your group has medical training – perhaps they can take responsibility for a group kit. If not, it's well worth doing a basic first-aid course and learning CPR techniques, wound care and how to handle choking and breathing emergencies before embarking on any serious camping trip or 4WD adventure.

Consider having multiple kits – what you carry for a short solo hike will be less comprehensive than a first-aid kit for an extended group camping trip.

Some other useful items to have in your emergency kit are:

- ☐ emergency whistle – old school but a lifesaver when lost

- ☐ emergency fire-lighting kit – ferro rod (*see* p. 129), fire strike, waterproof matches in a sealed plastic canister

- ☐ water filters, water purification tablets or a SteriPEN

- ☐ personal locator beacon – to send your location data to the authorities in an emergency

- ☐ solar hand crank or battery-powered radio for emergencies

- ☐ paracord – handy as an extra guy line, or for bundling wood, hanging provisions away from animals and building a shelter in an emergency.

Pack all of these items into a waterproof sack.

Important but non-essential items
Matting
Camping can be a grubby experience and keeping your tent and sleeping area clean makes a big difference. Bring a mat for your tent entrance and remind everyone to take off their shoes before coming in.

If you're camping on sandy, dusty or gravel surfaces, large mesh matting (usually 6m × 3m or larger) is helpful in keeping the sand and dirt out of your campsite, trailer or tent. It's made of a clever weave that allows sand and dirt to fall through the mat to the ground underneath. It's a bit like a giant picnic blanket that everyone can relax on, and it provides a safe place for the kids to play. Ideal for use in your communal area.

Dustpan and brush/broom
An absolute must for an orderly camp and harmonious tent!

Portable toilet
I would say this is practically an essential for remote travel these days. They're cheap and efficient and take care of human waste with ease.

Eye mask and earplugs
Recommended if you're light- or sound-sensitive (or festival camping!). Personally, I'm an early riser and love the dawn chorus, but here in Australia it can be really intense!

Portable power bank/battery
A lot of modern gear needs power and you don't want to drain your vehicle's battery. Portable power is reducing in price and increasing in efficiency. It will happily charge laptops, phones, cameras or power your lighting system. The larger ones can be

charged from 240V (120V USA). Add a solar panel set-up for the ultimate in portable power.

Hygiene

The perception that camping means being feral is one of the turn-offs for many potential campers. It really doesn't need to be this way.

While you can easily create a 'camper's bath' with a bucket, sponge and a minimal amount of hot water mixed with cold, these days there are plenty of portable solar shower solutions. They can be easily rigged up to hang from your vehicle and the water is heated by the sun's warmth.

Beyond this, there are more luxurious units that are powered by 12V or lithium batteries, with the water heated by a gas cylinder. If you have room and are on a long trip, these are well worth the investment.

Tarp

A tarp is simply a piece of material that can be erected or pitched in multiple configurations. You can either use poles as supports or 'fly' the tarp over a ridge line (usually a length of rope) and use guy ropes from various tie-down points to tension the tarp.

A tarp is a great centrepiece to your campsite that everyone can relax under. It can be used as an extra shade structure over the top of your tent set-up, or as a groundsheet in place of a picnic blanket. We often have the kitchen set up under a tarp. When it's raining people can gather there, and it offers shade from the midday sun.

Tarps come in many shapes, sizes and materials, all of which have different advantages and disadvantages. Depending on the size of the tarp and the material, you may need heavy poles, but if aluminium poles are sufficient they make your kit lighter. There's a bit of a learning curve with pitching and tensioning a tarp, but it's well worth the effort.

Binoculars

Binoculars (and monoculars) are great for birdwatching, stargazing, hunting or even just getting a better look at your glorious surroundings. A decent pair of binoculars will enhance your time out in nature and are a lot of fun for kids.

Cleaning and other important bits

It should go without saying that you need a cleaning kit for washing-up and waste disposal. Biodegradable soap and sponges are a must. I like to use collapsible folding washing tubs to save space. I take one for washing and another for rinsing.

Aluminium foil, cling wrap or more environmentally aware alternatives, like beeswax wraps, will always find a use around camp. Other necessities are ziplock bags, cable (zip) ties and gaffer tape. It's surprising how often you'll use these for various reasons.

Insect repellents

Insect bites can absolutely ruin your time out in nature and can also have severe and long-lasting consequences. Depending on where you plan to travel, you may be exposed to mosquitos or ticks that spread any number of diseases like dengue fever, Lyme disease, Rocky Mountain spotted fever (RMSF), or the zika virus. These are threats not to be taken lightly, so you should do your research before you leave.

While it's preferable to use natural products, sometimes they're ineffective. DEET and picaridin are the most well-known and effective repellents available. You can soak gear (clothing, tents, sleeping bags and other outdoor gear) in permethrin, which is an insect repellent and insecticide that kills ticks, mosquitoes, spiders, chiggers, mites and many other kinds of insects. Permethrin is also effective against the yellow fever mosquito that spreads the zika virus. You should research the pros and cons of these chemicals first.

Oil of lemon eucalyptus is the most effective of the natural insect repellents and the only one I use. Most other natural products are not particularly effective.

In Australia and other countries, flies can be a major hassle at certain times of the year. A head net with an insect shield could be considered an essential item and is, I think, preferable to coating your skin with DEET.

Storage

As you can see, particularly with car camping, there's a lot of gear to transport. Being organised makes the whole experience much more enjoyable. Naturally, having all the gear and the right storage that works for you is something to work towards, and when you're a beginner you'll often just make do with whatever you have at hand. Ideally, you'll eventually invest in some good quality tubs to transport your kit.

TUBS AND BOXES

Look for tubs that are as durable as possible. A lot of the cheaper ones won't make it through your first trip! They should seal well and have strong lids that lock into place and won't break when stacked on top of each other.

The size and type of tub that you use will depend on your vehicle. Measure up your boot (trunk) or cargo area and work out what will be the best fit before you buy. Often multiple smaller tubs are better than one large tub as they're easier to manage. You might consider tubs in a variety of sizes to accommodate different sized items, for example larger tubs for bulky gear. It makes sense to separate your gear into related items – kitchen, pantry, lighting, tools, and so on. And it's a good idea to label your tubs, or use colour-coded lids or stickers that describe the contents.

Plastic milk crates are totally underrated and excellent for camping. They're cheap, sturdy, lightweight and stack easily. You can also see what's in them. You can sit on them or use them as a side table. You can use them as an extra step to access your vehicle roof. You can stow jerry cans or gas bottles in them, then safely tie them to your roof rack system. In other words, they are extremely versatile!

Some plastic tub brands are specifically made to store cargo on your vehicle roof. They'll be made from a thick rotomolded plastic, weather-sealed, stackable, have strong handles and be durable enough to handle the pressure of ratchet straps or tie downs.

Small multi-compartment plastic boxes or tool boxes can be used for other handy items, like bottle openers, fishing hooks, sewing kits, small tools, rubber bands and other miscellaneous items.

BAGS

Use small canvas bags or pouches to create specialist kits of related gear, like condiments, coffee, first-aid, tools, pegs and mallet, and so on. Use a canvas utensil/tool roll to protect knives.

Contractor (or tradesperson) bags, used by tradespeople on building sites, are handy for camping storage. They have a rugged design with tough handles and loads of internal and external pockets and compartments – excellent for storing miscellaneous gear in.

Large canvas tote bags are also a good idea. You can see their contents easily, and they're quick to access and easy to carry. Large duffel bags are ideal for clothing and other soft goods. You can find weather-resistant duffels that have strong webbing handles and lashing points – perfect for a camping trip!

Slings, belt bags, bumbags or fanny packs – whatever you want to call them – are really handy for keeping small essentials – keys, wallet, flashlight, insect repellent and sanitiser – on hand, both around camp and in your vehicle.

Dry bags

A waterproof bag with roll-top closure that seals watertight is worth its weight in gold for hiking trips, and is just as useful for car camping. It makes for a great emergency kit bag, so that you can safely stow gear that needs to stay dry in a storm situation, like a fire-lighting kit, sleeping bag, clothing and electronics.

Other organisers

Canvas car seat organisers are bags that hang on the back of the front car seat, and are brilliant! They have a myriad of pockets of varying shapes and sizes, with compartments for pens, maps, phones or random kids' toys.

4WD rubbish bin bag

This is one for 4WD owners. It's a really handy and often overlooked item that solves a big problem with remote camping where rubbish disposal can be difficult. It's a soft rubbish bin, usually made from PVC or canvas (or both). It secures to the spare wheel or tailgate of your vehicle so that when you're transporting rubbish after camping it won't pollute the inside of your vehicle. It's also a good place to store wet clothes or other gear you don't want inside.

Preparing for a car camping trip

Get to know your gear before heading off. Set up your tent at least once before departing and note the best way to pack and unpack it. Make sure that you have your poles, pegs and mallet – it's often best to have these in a separate bag, rather than rolled inside a tent where you can't see them.

Check all gear that has been in storage to make sure everything is there, batteries are charged and there are no missing parts. Pay special attention to crucial gear like your first-aid kit. Test your stove and lighting before you leave. Make sure you have backup fuel and batteries for your devices.

FOOD

Plan your meals in advance and, if possible, prep as much food as you can beforehand. Simply add up your breakfasts, lunches and dinners, write a menu, then plan your shopping around it. Add in extra dried goods – like rice, beans and pasta – plus some cans of baked beans, spaghetti, tomatoes and tuna so that you have extra, just in case. I like to have pre-cooked meals like curries or stews on hand. These are perfect for the first night when it's generally quite hectic and you'll want to have something quick and easy. From there you'll have a bit more time for that juicy steak or roast you've been planning.

Taking whole foods – like vegetables, fruits and cured meats – reduces the load in your cool box. Apples and oranges travel well. And I generally take a lot of root vegetables – potatoes, onions, carrots, squash, artichokes and parsnips – and thick-skinned varieties of zucchini (courgette), eggplant (aubergine) and cucumbers that will last well in most conditions. Who doesn't love roast jacket potatoes cooked on a campfire?

Ingredients or premixes for simple camp bread – bannock bread, damper and pancakes – are quick and easy to make and always go down well. Oats are a popular alternative to eggs for brekky. Flat breads, like corn tortillas or other unleavened wraps, fried with cheese and whatever stuffings you prefer, are handy quick meals around camp. They're easy to transport and have a decent shelf life.

Cured meats, smoked fish and hard cheese are a great source of protein and a favourite that can be laid out at short notice to feed the team. Chorizo, cured bacon, sausages and fresh eggs are a must for your camping breakfast. Nothing beats campfire bacon and eggs out in the bush.

Butter, oils and condiments can be packed into small containers or mini travel bottles. Tiny sealable stainless steel containers are perfect for salt, pepper and other spices.

Dehydrated or freeze-dry packet meals have come a long way and some are actually really good. On a long trip (anything more than a week) I take a small bucket with a dozen meals. I rarely use them but they're handy to have on hand for an emergency, and are good for taking on hikes. They last a few years.

Don't forget chocolate or something sweet. This will always go down well around a campfire as an after dinner treat.

Pack food into resealable ziplock bags or sealed containers. Even better, use a vacuum sealer (a worthwhile investment in my opinion). Pack dry food into smaller containers that will fit snugly into larger tubs. Put everything that needs to stay cool in a cooler – make sure you have enough ice bricks ready before you set off. It's a good idea to pack things in the cooler in the order you'll need them, and keep an extra cool bag on hand for refreshing beverages!

GEAR CHECKLIST

'A place for everything and everything in its place.'
– origin unknown

Create or download a checklist of the essentials and non-essentials that you want to take (*see* pp. 31–76). Make sure it's tickable! Be honest with yourself about what you really need to take. Non-essentials should be reduced as much as possible. Prioritise items that have more than one use.

Give yourself plenty of time to pack. Preferably do it at least the day before, as trying to get kit together in a rush will lead to stress and potential failure.

Lay everything out in one place and group the items together in their logical categories before putting them into their tubs or bags. Once you have all your gear and luggage together, move this near to the rear of your vehicle before you start loading in.

PACKING YOUR VEHICLE

Don't be tempted to randomly throw everything into your vehicle.
Think about the order in which you'll want to use various items.
The first gear packed should be the gear that you need last and
vice versa. If you're planning to arrive at camp fairly late then it
makes sense to have your tent easily accessible as you might need
to set this up before dark or if inclement weather comes rolling in.
You'll be looking to maximise all space but still remain safe, so
load your vehicle with heavier tubs spread evenly so that you're
not overloading specific areas.

Pack your vehicle systematically with flat heavy boxes first
and layers of lighter gear, like bags and bedding, on top. Use
the vehicle floor space for bags and fill any holes with sleeping

bags and soft items. Items that you'll need to access easily should be on hand. Take a spare set of car keys, extra torch (flashlight), fire-starting kit and waterproof jacket and keep them somewhere safe and easy to access, like your glove compartment. Double-check that you'll have easy access to your first-aid kit at all times.

ROOF RACK SYSTEMS

There are literally hundreds of roof rack systems ranging from basic bars to elaborate platforms, or trays that are designed with campers in mind and have clever modular systems and channels for stowing specific items. At the very least, even if you have a small sedan vehicle, you could inexpensively fit a cargo box or bag that will give you much-needed extra storage space.

If you're packing onto a roof rack system, you need to be conscious of how much weight you have on top. The less weight the better as it can severely affect your vehicle's centre of gravity. Your vehicle manufacturer will have a maximum roof load rating and you'll need to consider how much you're adding to your roof, including the roof rack system itself. Most 4WDs can handle 100–200kg (220–440lb). This is why aluminium is the best choice for roof rack systems as it's light and strong. Each component of your roof storage system will also have a maximum rating, so be conscious of this.

Learning how to use ratchets (cargo-securing straps with a lock) and tie downs makes the roof a secure place to transport bulky items, such as swags, sleeping pads, tables and tents. Cage or basket-style platforms offer plenty of places to tie down. Add to this a large roof bag that can be attached using ratchet and cable (zip) ties and you can stow away a lot of gear with minimal struggle.

Most 4WDs have more weight towards the rear axle and less towards the front. If you add a full cargo bay, your vehicle can easily become overloaded. So aim to offset the weight by packing more weight towards the front on your roof rack system.

You'll often see fuel, portable toilets and LPG gas bottles on top of roof racks. This is because they are either unsafe to pack inside your 4WD, or they smell!

STAY SAFE

Packing your vehicle safely is an absolute priority. Ensure that heavy items won't be a risk to yourself or passengers in the event of an accident. Often cargo bays and car boots will have D rings and anchor points for ties downs so that you can secure tubs and heavy items with strapping.

If you have an SUV or 4WD with a cargo bay I strongly recommend a cargo barrier that separates the cargo back from the passenger seats and is designed to stop your gear flying forward if you're in an accident. Cargo barriers will usually be made from steel mesh (a bit like a cage), so you can use tie downs to anchor your storage tubs and heavy equipment to the barrier.

Weight can negatively affect your vehicle's handling performance and tyre usage as well as fuel consumption, so understanding how best to distribute weight is key. All cars will have a maximum weight when fully loaded. This will include the weight of the car, fuel, your gear and your passengers. It's known as Gross Vehicle Weight (GVW) or Gross Vehicle Mass (GVM). You can find your car's figure in the owner's manual or online (forums are a good place to look). If in doubt, you can weigh your loaded vehicle at the nearest public weighbridge.

Ideally, you should pack your vehicle so that you're still able to see out of your rear-view mirror. If your sight is restricted you can use your side mirrors, but make sure they're set properly.

Camping with kids

Camping with kids is a wonderful experience. The kids love it, you all get away from the daily routine (and screens!) and it encourages plenty of exploring, connecting with nature and imagining.

We took our first family camping trip when our eldest child was about one. If you're new parents, I recommend camping either before your baby can crawl, or after they start walking. In my experience with our second child, it's a bit of a hassle dealing with a baby crawling through the dirt, and is much more enjoyable when they're on two feet.

While camping with kids is a lot of fun, it pays to be as prepared as possible to make it the best experience it can be. So, here's a list of tips to get you started.

WHAT TO PACK

Along with everything else you'll be packing for your camping trip (*see* pp. 31–76), I recommend you also consider the following when bringing along little ones.

- Clothes – a great hack for packing camp clothes for kids is rolling up a whole day's outfit together and tying a band around it. This means there's less rummaging through bags and it's easy for kids to dress themselves! Make sure to pack items that are rugged and hard-wearing, as one thing is guaranteed – the kids will be covered in dirt in no time.

- Backpacks for each child – packed with a water bottle, lunchbox, whistle attached (just in case!), sunscreen, hat, special toys, and so on. Get the kids to help pack their own backpacks before the trip, taking some responsibility for their own belongings.
- Headlamp and glowsticks – giving them their own headlamp gives them a feeling of autonomy (glowlights are also endlessly fun, as well as practical).
- Baby wipes and hand sanitiser are both essential, especially when camping remotely with no showers or handbasins.
- In case of bad weather, make sure you have some games and activities packed to use inside the tent or under the tarp, like card games, colouring sheets and books. Try to avoid anything with very small pieces, like Lego or puzzles, as these can be easily lost.
- Food – think about how you can get the kids involved in camp cooking, which is all part of the experience. Easy stuff for kids to help cook includes veggies and sausages on a grill over the fire, and of course toasted marshmallows for dessert. I recommend packing decent lunch boxes for the kids to use on any trips away from camp. Stackable tiffin tins (inexpensive stainless steel lunch boxes from India) are great for this purpose.

CHOOSING A CAMPSITE/LOCATION

Think carefully about your kids' ages and what they'll enjoy doing while camping. If you're camping in hotter months, obviously somewhere near water is great as water play will take up much of the day! Fishing is another fun, low-fuss activity kids can get involved with.

Also, think about the types of facilities you want available at the campsite to make your life easier! Do you want a running shower and proper toilets, or are you happy with roughing it a bit more? Consider whether you want to be near other families for the social aspect, or somewhere that is more remote and secluded for some quality family time.

What about your campfire and its proximity to the tent? Some campsites will have a designated fire pit right in front of your tent, others will have communal fire pits further away. It's something to consider when putting young kids down to sleep while you stay up longer – you'll still want to be close by.

GETTING THERE

Most places worth camping at will likely be a fair drive away from where you live. Try to engage the kids beforehand on where you're going – like showing them a map and some photos – to keep them interested along the way. Think about your playlist or audiobooks when on the road.

Stop often for stretches and snacks and show the kids how far is left to go on the map. Allow ample time in your plans for these impromptu stops as it can add a lot of time to your journey. For example, if you estimate that it is a two-hour drive to camp, add at least an hour to your planning!

WHEN YOU ARRIVE

Try to arrive at your campsite with plenty of daylight left, allowing you time to set up camp, start a fire and get dinner organised. Have pre-dinner snacks ready to go for arrival at the campsite. There's nothing worse than trying to get set up and prepare dinner in the dark with hungry kids!

If you know you're going to arrive late in the day, pack a pre-cooked dinner that just needs heating up.

GET THEM INVOLVED!

Once you arrive at the campsite, get your kids to help set up. Give them small and manageable age-appropriate tasks. Our kids love collecting sticks and leaves for the campfire, and this activity can keep them busy for ages.

Depending on age, setting regular daily/nightly jobs for the kids is a great way to give them a sense of accomplishment and contribution to the camp. For example, it can be someone's job to collect fresh water, set up the camp chairs or help prepare dinner.

CAMP ETIQUETTE

It's important for kids to know the ground rules when it comes to camping with others, taking care of the campsite and being responsible for their safety. Make sure to explain some basic camp etiquette and rules when you arrive:

- Tell them not to run through other people's campsites.
- Remind them to keep quiet after waking in the morning (not everyone gets up at the crack of dawn!).
- Set boundaries around the campsite for where you're happy for them to explore.
- Educate them on fires and how to keep safe around them.
- Explain that the camp needs to stay neat and tidy (just like at home, right?!).

To make communication fun, you could bring walkie talkies. Having glowsticks for the kids is also a great way to keep track of them when the sun goes down. They will love them too!

Camping with dogs

It can be very hard to leave your best mate behind when going on holiday, not to mention the expense of a kennel, but luckily many public and private campsites will allow you to bring your canine companion. Depending on what country you live in, you might even be able to take your furry friend to a national or state park. There are no hard and fast rules, and there will be different guidelines depending on your location. Ring ahead and check with your local authorities first.

Some commonsense rules are:

- Your dog will need to be with you at all times. You can never leave a dog unattended at camp. Unfamiliar surroundings, the smell of a neighbour's barbecue, and local wildlife and other dogs mean it's easy for dogs to get distracted and wander.

- You'll probably need to have your dog on a leash, or at least have a leash on hand at all times. Take some extra long chain so that you can tie your dog up but have enough length for it to roam around camp.

- Dogs will need to wear a collar with an ID tag at all times.

- Dogs should be well trained and responsive to basic obedience commands like 'stay' and 'leave it!' – handy when dealing with wild animals like snakes.

- Depending on where you're camping, paralysis ticks and other insects can be a menace to your dog. Do your research and take preventative measures before setting out.

- Bring a dog crate just in case they need some time out.

- Generally, it's advised to have your dog sleeping in your tent or car where there's less likelihood of a confrontation with a wild animal.

- Bring some home comforts, like a dog bed. It will be easier to settle your dog at night.

- Make sure you pick up dog waste and dispose of it in the correct way.

- The heat and energetic excitement can quickly lead to dehydration, so keep your dog cool and watered.

- If your dog is prone to barking a lot don't bring them camping.

4

Campsites

Choosing where to camp

When it comes to picking your destination, learning what to
look for and what to steer clear of is a crucial part of ensuring an
enjoyable camping experience. Firstly, you need to figure out what
kind of camping you're doing: established campground camping
which will offer some amenities, or more remote 'primitive'
camping which is usually without people nearby, no access to
a bathroom, running water, electricity and, likely, no mobile
phone reception.

The internet can offer a fountain of great information, but local
knowledge and in-the-know friends are the best resources for
finding the *right* spot.

Established campgrounds

If you've only camped once or twice before, plan to stay in an established campground in an official camping area. National parks or state forests are a good bet.

An established camping site will often have amenities like a designated fire pit and picnic table. They may also have toilets (most probably a long drop) and, if you're lucky, showers.

For popular campsites, especially during the school holidays, you'll need to be organised well in advance. Some campsites may have a 'first come first served' policy for allotted sites. You can try your luck, but it pays to be the early bird.

Research and read reviews online. Usually, you can find good campsites that are near the area you want to visit that aren't overcrowded because they're an extra 20 minutes away, or don't have that shower block. If you're travelling at peak times this is often worth it to avoid crowds.

Check to see what sort of road leads into the campsite and if your car can handle the conditions. Make sure to check whether you can drive your car up to the campsite too – otherwise you'll have to carry your gear in.

Check conditions before you leave. You'll want to be prepared for both the weather and the environment you'll be camping in. Arrive well before sundown – the earlier the better, to avoid setting up camp in the dark.

Back-country camping

For more experienced campers, a remote location will give you greater opportunity for seclusion. It's a fantastic way to experience nature's gifts and means you're not dependent on campsite facilities and other people. This creates a heightened sense of self-reliance and resilience.

This sort of camping is not without its challenges. It takes more planning and preparation to ensure that you have adequate provisions, water and fuel. And it requires the right vehicle to ensure a safe trip.

PREPARING FOR A BACK-COUNTRY TRIP

'If you fail to plan, you are planning to fail!'
– Anonymous

'Proper Planning and Preparation Prevents Piss Poor Performance.'
– Anonymous

Before heading off, some campers prepare a precise itinerary including every last detail; others prefer a rough outline of the trip with plenty of room for ad hoc adventures. If you're travelling with kids you want to reduce travel times as much as possible and also ensure you're arriving at camp with plenty of sunlight left.

Word of mouth from a good source is a great way to find the campsite of your dreams. So ask friends and family for recommendations or, even better, talk to a ranger in the area you're aiming for. Backpacking and outdoor online forums are excellent resources for finding reviews of areas and getting an understanding of the site's conditions. There are also many good websites that will provide up-to-date information and reviews of campsites, local landmarks and hikes.

Once you have a basic outline of where you plan to go, you need to get an understanding of what facilities will be available. This is where guide books and online research comes in. Once you have a basic route which incorporates key locations you want to visit and any side trips, you can add this to a spreadsheet in the order of your tour. This is a great way to record key information, including travel times, things to see, number of nights you plan on staying, booking information and expectations for fuel, water and food consumption, and availability for stocking up. This will give you an overall picture of your trip, and you can easily add and remove locations to gain an understanding of different scenarios.

When you've nailed your itinerary, you can upload it to one of the many online services which will allow you to share it to an app.

YOUR VEHICLE

Is your vehicle up to the job? An honest appraisal of your transportation and its condition is crucial. If you're travelling in areas with no supplies you'll need a vehicle that's big enough to accommodate extra food, water and fuel and still be safe to drive with 360-degree vision and heavy objects stored securely in your cargo space or on the appropriate roof rack.

TOWING A TRAILER

If you're towing a trailer make sure your vehicle has the necessary towing capacity. You'll need to check the maximum weight your vehicle can tow, and the correct tow ball load specification (the amount of downwards pressure that can be applied to the rear of the towing vehicle). This is measured as a proportion of the weight of the trailer, for example, 10 per cent. Taking a trailer or camper-trailer over rough terrain should not be taken lightly. Thorough research should be done before you head into the back-country with a trailer.

DRINKING WATER

Make sure you have more than adequate drinking supplies for your trip. This will most likely mean taking a lot of water with you, as you can't always guarantee that water in the wild is safe to drink. Remember to take a water filter (*see* p. 53).

FUEL

Planning your fuel consumption is essential to a successful trip into the back-country. You'll need to check fuel stops along the route and calculate your reserve requirements. A vehicle that runs on diesel will often be the most efficient for a long-range trip.

ROAD CONDITIONS

What is the condition of the roads or tracks for your route? If you're planning on driving on unmade and uneven terrain a 4WD is recommended and may be the only acceptable form of transportation for that route. You should always check in with the national parks or other advisory authorities about road conditions before leaving. Roads and tracks can be closed for many reasons, from fire and snow to grading or other repair works.

PERMITS

If you're planning to camp in national parks or other protected areas outside of a designated campsite you may need a permit. Check with the appropriate authorities first.

If you're out in the back-country, choose a campsite near a river or other water source. Apart from giving you access to fresh drinking water (make sure you boil it first!), you'll also have a place to bathe and a water source for washing-up, cooking and dousing fires. You shouldn't use soap and detergents in rivers and lakes as this can pollute the environment and potentially harm wildlife. If you've got kids with you, be mindful of fast-flowing water.

CHOOSING A SITE

When you arrive at your destination, if there's a choice of campsite select one carefully. If you're at an organised campsite, note potential neighbours – sometimes there are campers you'll want to avoid. Use your powers of discernment to decide who will be a good neighbour.

Study the features of the campground, like the surrounding shade area and access to tracks and roads. If you have a choice, avoid traffic. Aim to camp as close as possible to a water source but not too close to the bathroom facilities, as they attract heavy traffic and can produce unwelcome odours. Choosing a site that's at least a short walk away will provide a much-needed bad-smell buffer zone.

If you're foraging for firewood it makes sense to camp near a wooded area. Make sure you don't obstruct any paths or tracks, and that your entry and exit are likely to be clear at all times in case of an emergency.

SETTING UP CAMP

The first thing to do after arriving at a campsite is to think about the layout of the camp. If you're camping in a group you should decide on a common area – usually near a campfire. From there, you can decide on the kitchen area, where the tents will be set up and the pit toilet, if required. If there's a view, it makes sense to orientate the common area and the front of your tents towards it.

Plan these spaces by laying your gear out on the ground. Try to keep your cooking, eating and washing-up areas well away from your tent.

Keep in mind where the sun rises and sets in relation to any shade, as this will determine how early you wake and how hot your tent is in the afternoon. You may be an early riser or want your tent to dry quickly in the morning, so it makes sense to have the door facing east and not have the tent in a shaded spot.

If there's a persistent wind direction look for some sort of natural windbreak, like bushes or boulders. If you're camping in an open space you can position your vehicle as a windbreak.

Avoid camping in old, dry riverbeds or gullies that could flood, even if it seems an impossibility that there will be rain. Flooding can come from a weather event a long way upstream.

Valley bottoms and depressions are prone to cold, humid air, so even a slight elevation will usually be dryer and warmer. Look for a level piece of ground near a slope, so water can run off in the event of rain. As much as you want shade, avoid camping under a tree – falling branches, the potential for lightning strikes, critters and insects can make this hazardous.

Unpack systematically and set up your shelter first. Choose a flat spot on which to pitch your tent. Remove any debris – like rocks or sticks – that could damage your groundsheet or make for an uncomfortable stay. Avoid areas that could be flooded from run-off in a storm. Pace out the size of your tent, making sure you have plenty of room on all sides for the guy ropes. Once your tent is set up, place your bedding inside, then set up the rest of the camp.

Ideally, try to have your kitchen close to a water source. Set up at least one designated rubbish bin and a tub for recycling. A tarp is a brilliant centre point for a camp, offering protection from both the sun and rain. It can be the best place for your kitchen and daytime communal area. It has open sides so it can be easily accessed from all directions, and it keeps everyone together during camp chores, like preparing dinner.

If you're staying a while, set up a clothesline. It's guaranteed that it will be in constant use, especially if you have kids and are in proximity to water. If they're anything like mine, they'll be wet within minutes!

A fire pit is essential for the full camping experience. Cooking on an open fire is one of life's great culinary experiences, and the campfire will be your main source of light, heat and communal gathering. If possible, use an existing fire circle that past campers have left behind.

If you need to make one from scratch, choose an area of about 3m (10ft) in diameter that is free of flammable debris and grass. Bare soil, sand or gravel is best. If you have a camp shovel, dig out a shallow circle, about 1m (3ft) wide, and place rocks around the circumference of your pit to ensure your fire doesn't spread (*see* p. 133).

KEEP THINGS ORGANISED

Ensure you have a dedicated spot for essentials. For instance, I always put the spare car keys, head torch (flashlight) and some other important items in a pocket inside the tent (no point locking the keys in the car!) and this gives me peace of mind. I'll never forget one camping trip when we realised we'd lost our car keys. We spent that night and most of the next morning frantically looking for them, before resigning ourselves to hiking out to the main road to seek help. It was only when we'd packed down and rolled up the tent that we found the keys sitting there in the dirt!

Organising your campsite is key to having a relaxed experience. Camping is best enjoyed when everything has its designated place and is easy to find whenever you need it. Once it gets dark, you don't want to have to stumble around, tripping over random piles of equipment while you search in vain for this pot or that blanket.

If you're camping in the wild your camp needs to be kept tidy in order to reduce the chances of a wildlife invasion. Keep all food and food waste in sealed containers that critters and insects can't access. Store rubbish bins in a vehicle when you leave the campsite for the day or at night, as all sorts of animals and insects will be coveting your food scraps. If your campsite has bear boxes or other storage containers on-site, use them.

You and your campmates should strive to develop good camp routines and habits that everyone is aware of, like washing-up after eating, and returning tools and equipment to their designated space. Sweeping up your tent and communal areas keeps things fresh and orderly and encourages others to get involved in the camp maintenance. It's often good to designate tasks in a group camping situation and it's surprising how people will start stepping up to help out if you lead the way. Soon enough it becomes routine and your camp begins to operate smoothly!

A POO IN THE WILD

With so many people visiting remote areas, the days of pooing in the wild are rapidly disappearing. So if you're planning on a back-country trip with a vehicle, you should really invest in a portable toilet. But there will be times, like on a hike, when you find yourself without a portable toilet and you should be prepared.

Individual poos - cathole toilet

For individual poos when you're on the move, a cathole toilet will suffice. Simply dig a hole 15–20cm (6–8in) deep and 20cm (8in) wide with a camping trowel or spade and go about your business straddling the hole. Cover the hole on exit. Depending on the rules laid out for the area you're visiting, you should at least collect the toilet paper in a ziplock bag and dispose of it later.

Group poos - slit trench

If you find yourself without a toilet and are camping for multiple nights with a group of people, you may need to create a suitable trench latrine. The simplest and most efficient way to deal with group human waste is to have a single latrine that everyone uses. This isolates the waste which is better for the environment and better for other campers.

Before you begin

Look for a suitable level area at least 30m (98ft) away from your camp and, crucially, any water source.

Ideally, look for somewhere that is easy to access but well-screened with some privacy away from any track's foot traffic.

Try to find an area exposed to sunlight that will dry the waste quickly, making it easier to decompose. Look for deep, loose soil that will be easier to dig into.

The dig

Using a spade or other similar tool, like a trowel, dig a trench at least 15–20cm (6–8in) deep and 15cm (6in) wide and as long as you think you'll need for the time you're camping. A good rule of thumb is about 20cm (8in) per person per day.

Dig out the earth, creating a consistent ridge of dirt that runs parallel with the trench and is about 15cm (6in) from the edge.

In use

It's a good idea to brief your team on poo etiquette beforehand.

- Latrine users will straddle the trench, with one leg either side and then squat to do their business.

- Using a trowel or scoop, each person will use the loose earth on one side of the trench to cover their toilet waste which will aid decomposition (and is easier on the eye!).

- Make sure the group is aware that they should be starting at one end and progressing towards the other end of the trench, in sequence.

- A roll of toilet paper can be placed on a stick and stuck into the ground. It can be moved along as each person uses the latrine.

- Have a large ziplock bag on hand that can be used to collect the toilet paper.

- Have plenty of hand sanitiser available.

- Make sure you have a lantern or spare torch (flashlight) available for night-time activity.

- Use some sort of indicator that is near the entrance to the latrine area to indicate when it's in use. A hat on a stick or a trekking pole is a good way to prevent an awkward moment. If this is missing, it shows people that the latrine is in use.

- Having a support structure, like a branch or plank, running along the trench line helps people balance.

- Once the trench has been used a final time, fill it in with earth and cover with leaves to prevent wild animals digging it up.

How to hot tent: camping with a portable wood burning stove

WHAT IS A HOT TENT?

A hot tent is simply the use of a woodfire stove inside a tent set-up. It's essentially a firebox set on legs with the ability to draw in fresh air, burn fuel safely and efficiently, and exhaust the smoke and gas fumes outside the tent via a pipe (flue or chimney) system.

WHY HOT TENT?

Adding a heat source to your tent offers all sorts of possibilities when camping in cold conditions. You'll have a homely and welcoming base in which to stay comfortably for prolonged periods. Importantly, you'll have a warm space to dry wet clothing, boots and gear.

Being able to easily cook food and have hot water available inside your tent has obvious advantages. And being in a warm environment means you'll burn fewer calories, therefore needing less food. If it's sub-zero and inclement, stormy weather outside, starting an open fire can be difficult and time-consuming. Having a stove makes lighting a fire a straightforward process.

Aside from the practical reasons for creating a hot tent set-up, there's also the pleasing aesthetic of fire-gazing and the natural ambience created by a fire inside your tent. A hot tent provides you with uplifting respite away from the elements – a simple hot meal inside a cosy tent while it's pouring down outside is superb!

THE GEAR

There are many stoves that are suitable to use inside a tent, ranging from expensive but lightweight titanium stoves through to larger and stronger stainless steel or steel stoves.

Usually, there will be an adjustable air-intake vent set into the door opening which allows control of the oxygen drawn into the stove. To help regulate air flow there will be a damper mechanism within the stove exit section. In combination with the front air vent controls, dampers help adjust the fuel burn rate and so control heat by keeping it in the stove rather than letting it escape via the pipe system.

The chimney will exit the tent via a stove jack which is a fireproof-protected hole in either the tent wall or roof. The system will end with a spark arrestor section which is a device that prevents the emission of flammable debris and reduces the risk of burning the outer tent.

Some accessories available are hot water tanks (having hot water on tap is also a game changer), attachable ovens (pizza or fresh bread anyone?) and a built-in thermometer (always handy).

Large tents are best suited for hot tenting as you can keep more distance between yourself and the stove. Cabin or wall tents are often used for hot tenting in the United States and Canada for winter hunting expeditions. With the correct precautions, tipis, yurts, and bell, esker and laavu tents are good options but you should check compatibility with the manufacturer.

THE RISKS

Having a red-hot stove in your tent presents real risks which should not be taken lightly. You'll need to evaluate your gear (and competence level) for this type of camping. These risks can be reduced by doing your own research and taking a commonsense approach to safety precautions.

The most obvious risk is fire. I recommend camping in a tent that has been suitably fireproofed. Either the canvas itself should be woven from a fire-resistant material or the tent should be coated. Lightweight tents tend to be made from nylon and you'll need to pay special attention to how they're constructed for use with a stove. Ask the manufacturer if they're compatible.

You'll need to consider how the stove chimney exits the tent, either via a built-in exit jack or a hole made in your tent using a silicone flashing kit. The area where your stove pipe exits the tent should be made of a fireproof material panel (best option) or treated with a fireproof coating.

The hot stove pipe needs to be prevented from coming into contact with your tent canvas. This is usually done by incorporating a double-pipe section in the set-up. I also recommend a spark arrestor on the last section of pipe chimney which will keep your tent protected from any errant sparks that make their way up the chimney system.

Probably the most common danger in hot tenting is being burned by the stove itself. I recommend placing the stove on a fireproof mat and, if possible, incorporating a fireguard into your set-up. Don't handle the stove or other parts without wearing fireproof gloves (welder's gloves are useful). When you position the stove, think about where it is in relation to the tent door and access to the rest of the tent.

The danger of carbon monoxide poisoning is not to be underestimated. This occurs when exhaust fumes escape from your stove system into the tent. This can happen either because there's some sort of blockage in the pipes or because a strong wind is blowing directly into the exit pipe. Carbon monoxide is odourless and colourless and so difficult to detect. For this reason, I don't recommend sleeping with your stove lit, and you should invest in a battery-operated carbon monoxide alarm.

Stoves need oxygen to burn, so it's important to provide plenty of ventilation in your tent while it's in action. What's more, condensation will build from your breath, and having the windows or door slightly open will reduce this problem.

OTHER TIPS

It makes sense to find a location that will give you some protection from high wind. If you're camping in snow, you can either dig out the snow or flatten it to create a smooth, flat platform before pitching your tent.

Keep a supply of dry wood inside the tent as you'll want to have a fire first thing in the morning. Having a clothesline that can be strung across the tent's interior is a great way to dry out clothes that will inevitably be damp from the day's activity. If you're camping in cold conditions it should go without saying that you need the appropriate sleeping bag and sleeping pad (not an air mattress!).

5

Wood and fire

Ancient campfire

Somewhere between 400,000 and 1.5 million years ago, humans discovered how to manipulate fire. This revolutionary technology would have triggered a huge upgrade in our ancestors' living standards. I've often wondered about how harsh life must have been without it. No comforting warmth on a cold night, no protection from dangerous animals, no light after sundown, and only raw food for dinner. Miserable!

It's no surprise that an open fire evokes a primal emotion within us. In my opinion, a fire is essential when you're spending a night in the bush, and it's one of the main reasons to go camping in the first place. An open fire does more than ward off the dark and any inquisitive animals. It's the heart of the campsite, a communal place where we gather to stay warm, cook food and share stories.

Up until the mid-20th century, lighting and maintaining a fire was a skill that almost everyone had, given that burning wood (or compressed wood as coal) was the main source of heating throughout the world. In modern times, most people no longer build a daily fire. Instead, warmth is magically pumped into their homes at the push of a button via a gas or electric heating system.

Building a campfire is a basic and rewarding skill that anyone and everyone should be able to master. It starts with finding the right fuel.

Foraging for fuel wood

'Birch and fir logs burn too fast
Blaze up bright and do not last,
it is by the Irish said
Hawthorn bakes the sweetest bread.
Elm wood burns like churchyard mould,
Even the very flames are cold
But ash green or ash brown
Is fit for a queen with a golden crown.'
– Lady Celia Congreve, 'The Firewood Poem', *The Times*, 1930

Unless you plan on taking bulk wood with you, you'll no doubt be foraging for fuel wood for a campfire. Before you leave you should research the rules in the area where you're planning to camp. Chopping down a tree or collecting fallen branches isn't always legal, especially in national parks, so it pays to check before you leave.

It should go without saying that you'll want to look for dry, dead wood that you'll process into a combination of sizes for kindling and larger fuel logs. When wood has dried and its moisture and sap has evaporated, it's known as 'seasoned wood', as opposed to 'greenwood' (live wood) where internal moisture is at its maximum.

Ideally, you'll be on the lookout for a combination of softwoods and hardwoods. Softwoods to get the fire blazing, and hardwoods to carry it through the night and produce heat.

SOFTWOODS

Softwoods are usually evergreen trees, like conifers (cone-bearing trees) – cedar, pines, cypress, fir, spruce, even giant redwood. Softwoods are favoured for starting fires because they're easy to process into kindling. Well-seasoned softwood is usually easier to ignite than hardwoods and burns faster with a higher flame, thus producing more light for the campsite.

For cooking, softwoods are good for boiling or frying as they release their heat quickly. They also tend to produce more smoke, which can be beneficial if you have mosquitos around!

HARDWOODS

Hardwoods are usually deciduous flowering or evergreen trees and are much denser than softwoods. In the Northern Hemisphere, birch, maple, hickory, oak, beech and ash are popular hardwoods. In Australia, acacias and eucalypts – like red or blue gum, jarrah, box and ironbark – are evergreen hardwoods that shed their leaves throughout the year.

Hardwoods are preferred as the main source of fuel, particularly if the fire is a source of warmth throughout the night because most hardwoods burn cleaner, hotter and for much longer than softwoods. They have a lower flame and are less likely to produce sparks and pops, so there's less likelihood of accidentally setting something alight around the camp.

Hardwoods also produce better coals for cooking than softwoods, and are best suited to cooking slow roasts or braises. Because hardwood takes significantly longer to burn down to coals, you should factor this into your plans.

WHAT TO LOOK FOR

As long as you're in or near wooded areas it should be straightforward to find dead fallen trees, branches, limbs or twigs suitable for a fire. Look for wood that is clearly seasoned. Telltale signs include wood with bark that is partly or fully removed, that lacks vibrancy and has a grey appearance, and that has splits and cracks from the surface deep into the core.

Ideally, you're looking for wood that is both dead and off the ground for the simple reason that it's dryer. Look for branches from a dead tree that's fallen on top of a shrub or bush, sometimes known as 'standing wood'. Collecting small sticks and twigs from standing wood will be helpful for creating kindling.

Once you've found branches or limbs that appear to be dry, try striking the wood with another dry piece of wood. It should make a hollow, slightly ringing sound that indicates dryness. Wet wood makes a dull thudding sound when hit.

Not all wood is created equal. Each species will produce different amounts of radiant heat (measured in BTU or British thermal unit), they have different burn rates and flame heights. Over time you'll develop some local knowledge about what works best for you.

STANDING TREES

'Give me six hours to chop down a tree and I'll spend the first four sharpening the axe.'
– Anonymous

It is worthwhile looking for a small dead 'standing tree' – a tree that has died but not yet fallen. Look for a standing tree that is less than an arm's thickness and has completely shed its leaves and, ideally, most of its bark. The advantage with dead standing trees is that because they're vertical they're less exposed to rain and so less likely to be waterlogged and rotten. Avoid trees that are infested with termites or ants as they tend to take on water too.

Once you've found a suitable tree you can either chop into the wood with an axe (if it chips it's probably dry enough for a campfire) or cut into the trunk with a knife and check that it is dry to the touch. Try to push or pull the tree over. If this isn't possible, cut it down with a saw, rather than an axe, which will be more efficient.

Look for signs of nesting within tree hollows and be extra careful not to disturb any animals or insect populations that may use the tree as their home.

CHOPPING WOOD

'He that cuts his own wood is twice warmed.'
– proverb

Having lived in houses with fireplaces or wood heaters and houses without, I know which I prefer. There's a huge amount of satisfaction to be had from cutting and processing wood to a useful size and then stacking it neatly. Swinging an axe and splitting a log brings forth an almost primeval emotion. The advent of the axe must have been revolutionary!

On more than one occasion I've lived in a house where a wood fire has been the only source of heat, so learning how to chop wood was a skill that quickly developed through repetitive practice and necessity. But before we get carried away, the first part of processing wood is best done using a saw. Once you've collected your wood, you'll need to cut it into smaller logs, or 'rounds', that will be easier to split with an axe or hatchet.

Before you start processing wood, consider wearing protective gloves and eyewear (glasses, sunglasses or goggles). Make sure you're wearing sturdy footwear (preferably strong boots) and ensure that your footing is secure and stable at all times.

Sawing logs to size

In the absence of a sawhorse, use a long log or stump as a brace so that you can position your length of wood at a right angle elevated from the ground. Make sure you saw into the wood at a right angle (90 degrees) to the point of contact.

Before beginning, it's a good idea to examine the log you're about to process to see where the knots are. It's harder to chop logs with knots or irregularities as the grain around these knots will be tougher to split. If you find a knot in the length of wood you're processing, cut in close either side to make sure that each section of wood doesn't have a knot in the middle. This will come in handy later as you start to split and process the wood further.

Draw your saw back towards you a few times to make sure it bites into the wood and creates a straight guideline. Try not to force the saw by applying too much downward pressure, instead let the teeth do the work for you. Make sure your logs are cut to size to fit into your fire bed or wood stove. When in doubt, about

30–40cm (12–16in) is a good size. You can mark the length out on your log before you cut it to size. This will mean that you have good uniformity with your smaller rounds. You'll also want to make sure that the ends are cut evenly, resulting in a flat surface so that the log can stand vertical on a stump for splitting later.

Splitting wood with an axe or maul

The ideal tool for splitting log rounds into medium-sized logs is a splitting axe or a maul. The key difference between a splitting and a felling axe is that a splitting axe usually has a heavier and blunter head which is designed to split wood fibres along the grain, while a felling axe generally has a sharper blade designed to cut through the wood fibres. A maul is a heavier and blunter tool, a bit like a sledgehammer with a wedge-shaped head.

Standing position

If you're chopping wood in a standing position you'll need a raised flat surface or stump. In an ideal world, you'd have a dry stump between 30cm (12in) and knee height. If this isn't available, try to find a large downed tree lying in a horizontal position that has enough flat surface area to safely balance the log.

Place the log on top of the stump on the far side away from you, so that if you miss your axe head will definitely end up hitting the stump. Make sure the log is standing up straight and not about to fall over.

Take your time to get the right position – this is not a job that should be rushed. Before you begin swinging an axe, ensure that your axe swing will not be inhibited by other objects, like branches (or people!). Keep your feet shoulder-width apart, squarely facing the stump. Make sure your stance is weighted evenly, with your legs and arms slightly bent and fairly relaxed.

The swing

With your axe in both hands, hold the axe horizontally at waist level, using your dominant hand to grip the handle near to the axe head. The V of your hand should be facing away from you. Use your other (non-dominant) hand to grip the other end near to the handle.

Check the striking distance to the log by lining up your axe with the target and tapping the log in the spot that you're aiming for. Aim for existing cracks on the edge of the wood which will help direct your first strike and ensure that you're less likely to get your axe stuck in the round.

As you swing the axe back and up, extend your arms high over your head, straighten your legs, then rise up slightly on the balls of your feet to maximise the swing. When your hands and axe are at arms-length, directly overhead and at the top of the arc,

let the axe drop down towards the log with your eyes fixed steadily on the target. As you're doing this let your dominant hand slide down the handle to meet your other hand and apply some force on the downward stroke.

Chopping wood isn't about being aggressive. Accuracy and technique are far more important than brute force. Use the axe's weight to your advantage and let the tool do the work for you.

Kneeling position

If you're using a small axe – anything less than a 1kg (2.2lb) head and a handle that is less than 70cm (27in) in length – or you don't have a decent stump or log to work with, try splitting wood in a kneeling position.

Kneeling is a far safer way to split wood as you keep your legs and torso out of harm's way. Simply kneel two arm-lengths away from your target and then adjust your position until the bit of the axe reaches the target with your arms fully extended. Then follow the same routine swinging your axe up and letting it fall on the vertical log.

Split, and split again

Depending on the size of your logs, you may need to split them in half or into quarters. After splitting in half, reposition one half of your log on the chopping block and split that in half. Repeat with the other half of the log. Processing your logs into smaller and smaller sections will create kindling.

Kindling

Kindling is simply a small piece of dry wood that is either foraged or created with a tool. It's used as fuel for the early stages of making a fire. The process of creating kindling from larger pieces of wood is an essential skill that will help you easily build a fire. As previously mentioned, ideally you will be using seasoned softwood as it requires less effort to process and will be much easier to ignite.

Look for logs with straight grains and no knots. Use a secure, hard, even surface as your chopping block and use the kneeling position, which is the safest way to process kindling. With some know-how, a hatchet or small axe is the best tool for the job. A heavy duty and very sharp cleaver or nata (Japanese tool) or large knife are also options for creating kindling.

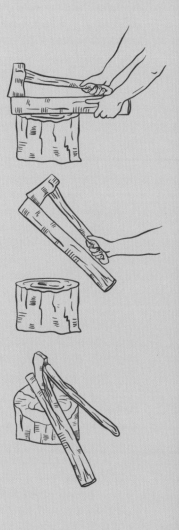

If you're using a small axe or hatchet, or are splitting long thin logs that are difficult to balance on a suitable surface, try splitting the wood horizontally. Find a limb of wood around the same length as your axe handle and about the thickness of an arm. Lay your log out horizontally with the far end resting on the stump or a hard surface. Tap your axe bit into the end of the log until it is embedded in the wood, then use the combined weight of the log and your attached axe to strike the hard surface.

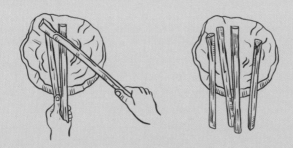

The axe will split into the log and then you can leverage and twist the split wood around the axe into two pieces. Continue this process until you have created enough small sections of split wood that can be used for kindling.

Batoning

Making and using a baton (a crude club-like tool) to help process wood is something that bushcraft folk love to debate at length, but it's a fairly basic concept. Batoning is simply using a suitable length of hardwood to drive a knife – ideally with a full tang (where the blade extends the full length of the handle) – through a small log, thus making the processing of kindling more efficient.

An ideal baton would be a found limb from a green hardwood tree that is about the thickness of a wrist, and around the length of your forearm and hand.

Feather sticks

Feather sticks are another favourite in the bushcraft world. A feather stick is made by using a blade (knife or hatchet) to shave down the length of a kindling stick to produce multiple curls of thin wood. With the right wood and a good technique, you'll end up with a piece of kindling that will have half its bulk shaved into curls at one end.

Because you're creating more surface area, this kindling ignites and spreads fire very quickly. This isn't just a fun thing to do, it can really help get a fire going quickly if you don't have much dry kindling around, particularly in wet weather.

What is tinder?

Tinder is the foundation of any fire. If you're not using fire starters and another 'helping-hand' fuel to start your fire, tinder is what you'll need for the job.

Tinder is simply refined and easily combustible material that will be used as a basic ingredient for igniting a fire. It's generally a fine, open, airy material that has a large surface area. Newspaper is perhaps the most commonly known form of tinder, but there are many options. They range from synthetics – like cottonwool and charcloth – to natural tinders – like finely processed bark, birds nest lint, dried lichen or moss, pine needles and fluffy seed heads of various weeds, like dandelion.

The type of tinder required will depend on the situation you find yourself in. If it's after dark on a stormy, wet night or you're in an emergency situation, you'll want to get your fire going with whatever is at hand as quickly as possible. This is where some pre-prepared tinder – usually in the form of a fire lighter! – is incredibly useful.

But if it's a hot day and there's plenty of dry material around, it'll be of little consequence if you haven't prepared tinder. As long as you have a way of igniting a fire, there'll be plenty of opportunities around the camp to find suitable material. Simply gather a bundle of thin dead twigs, shredded dried bark and dried grasses and form it into a bird's nest shape to use at the heart of your fire.

Natural tinder

If you're using a ferro rod (*see* p. 129) or fire strike you'll need material that will catch from a spark. It'll need to be dry and fluffy natural material.

Some natural forms of tinder that will take a spark and are highly prized by the bushcraft and survivalist community are:

- Chaga fungus – also known as tinder fungus or touchwood. It's a black bulbous fungus found on the birch tree in the Northern Hemisphere that's highly flammable once dried.

- Fatwood – found in the resinous heart of a pine tree stump. This is a brilliant natural fire accelerator and, if shaved thinly, it can take with a spark.

- Punk wood – dried or charred rotten wood that's been permeated by a mycelium fungus resulting in a light and spongy-textured wood that will take a spark and burn easily.

- Tree bark – the scrapings and shavings from the inner bark of many trees. Birch is the most popular, but cedar, cottonwood or poplar will also work.

These are useful to keep in a tinder box (sealed container). Along with a ferro rod, they would be welcome in any kit as part of an emergency fire-starting solution.

Synthetic tinder

There are a range of synthetic tinders available, like paraffin firelighters, but there are others you can make yourself:

- Cotton balls – dipped in petroleum jelly or wax.

- Charcloth – small squares of cotton cloth slowly heated to the point of pyrolysis (same process as charcoal) that can be stored in a sealed container for later use.

- Pine shavings – melted wax combined with pine shavings (tip: use a muffin tin as a mould).

- Clothes lint – wads of lint from a clothes dryer (tip: dip in wax or petroleum jelly for extra combustion!).

How to start a fire with a ferro rod

Sometimes referred to as either a fire starter, fire strike or fire steel (and not to be confused with a flint and steel), a ferro rod is a piece of man-made metallic material known as ferrocerium. When a ferro rod is scraped with a sharp object, like the spine of a knife, it'll shed quick-burning and hot sparks (over 3000°C or 5430°F) that can be used to light tinder.

Ferrocerium is the same combustible material used in most butane cigarette lighters and, with the exception of commercially made lighters or matches, is one of the most fail-safe tools for fire ignition. The reason ferro is so popular with campers and bushcraft enthusiasts is because of its simplicity. There's very little that can go wrong with a ferro rod. They work in freezing conditions (unlike butane), they won't break easily, are completely weatherproof and will last a long time (most manufacturers claim over 10,000 strikes!). It's a fun and impressive tool to use, and a good backup to have in any camping fire kit.

Ferro comes in various forms but is usually a rod with a handle made from plastic or wood (sometimes from bone or deer antler). There's a noticeable difference in the quality of available ferro rods and I recommend buying from a reputable manufacturer. Also, the larger the rod the better, as you'll have more of a striking area to work with. Some rods are sold attached to a knife, or come with a scraping tool or magnesium bar (another highly combustible material that will work from a strike).

To use a rod you'll need to strike it with a sharp, straight-edged metal tool. Carbon steel scraper tools are a good option, or you could simply use the spine (back) of a knife, ideally made from carbon steel with a flat 90-degree spine. Most camping or pocket knives will do the job and, contrary to myth, you can still get a spark using a stainless-steel edge. Please don't be tempted to use the knife blade. It will work but it will dull the knife's edge.

HOW TO USE

If you have a new ferro rod it will most likely be sealed with a black coating. This is to prevent the rod from oxidising and corroding. Using your scraping tool, scrape away at this coating a few times to reveal a silver surface. This is the exposed ferro, ready to use.

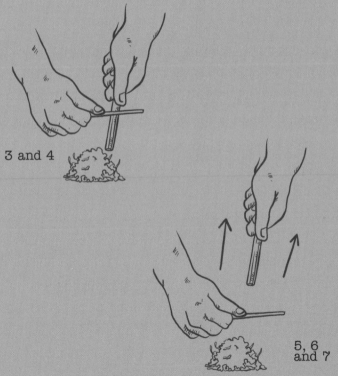

3 and 4

5, 6 and 7

STEPS

1. Have a basic campfire already set up and ready to light.
2. Choose your tinder – either foraged locally or previously prepared.
3. Make a bird's nest shape with your prepared tinder, placing larger material on the outside and finer tinder towards the centre.
4. Rest the tinder nest on a flat, dry surface – a slab of dry bark is ideal.
5. Hold the scraping tool over the nest at a 45-degree angle with the spine facing upwards.
6. Take your ferro rod and apply some pressure.
7. Slide the ferro rod perpendicular (right angle, 90 degrees) to the scraper towards you.

Note that the scraper is stationary and you're pulling the ferro rod across the edge of the scraper towards you. At first, this may feel wrong but it allows better directional control of the sparks.

Don't worry if at first you don't succeed. Try, and try again. It's really just practice and making sure that you have the right tinder for the strike.

The campfire

Planning and preparation are key to a successful campfire. Just like following a recipe and cooking a meal, there's a method that you need to follow. Certain stages will need to happen in a particular order, and there are specific ingredients you'll need in order to achieve a good campfire.

THE INGREDIENTS

Before you even think about striking a match, you'll need to have at least two fistfuls of the appropriate tinder (*see* p. 125), or some bunched or shredded paper if you have it, and an armful of dead and dry kindling of various sizes, from matchstick-thin kindling, through to larger sizes. For this stage of the fire the best kindling will be thin pieces you've cut to size or long, thin dead twigs and sticks from coniferous trees that break with a nice hollow clicking sound. You want a tangled bundle of twigs with plenty of surface area, much like a bird's nest.

Prepare some larger pieces of pencil-thin kindling and six larger pieces about two fingers thick. From here have hardwood logs in a range of different sizes, up to an arm's thickness. Gather all of your various sized pieces of wood and have them nearby.

How much fuel wood do you need for the job? More than you think! As a starting guide, have about a dozen average-sized logs – around 30cm × 15cm (12in × 6in) – which should be enough fuel for a dinner for four people. But it really depends on the type of wood that you're using and what you plan on cooking!

Always collect more wood than you think you'll need. Fires never go out because there's too much wood – it's always the opposite problem!

CONSTRUCTING A FIRE PIT

Most campsites will have fire pits or cleared patches of ground where others have set up campfires. If not, you'll need to prepare an area for a fire yourself.

Set up your fire well before dark so that you can see what you're doing. The process starts by selecting your campfire's location. Choose a location carefully. It should be clear of at least 1.5–3m (5–8ft) of any natural fuel, for example, dry grass that might catch alight. Your tent and bedding should be even further away. Check that you're not building a fire near a standing tree and that there are no overhanging branches. Take note of the prevailing wind direction and make sure your dining area is upwind of the fire and away from you as you cook.

If you're building on ground with thick forest litter – particularly in coniferous woodland – rake or scrape away the flammable organic material. Remove an area of soil around 10cm (4in) deep and 1m wide, or at least three times the size of the fire you intend to make. Don't build a fire on peat soil as it's possible to ignite the soil.

Once you've cleared the layer of turf, build a raised platform of dirt that is around 10cm (4in) in the centre of the cleared area. Ideally, ring the fire bed with large stones or cobbles. If there are enough stones available and you're staying a while, you could build a wall which encloses the fire on three sides, creating a hearth and windshield.

Ideally, you want to build a fire on flat, solid ground. Rock is the best choice but any sort of cleared area of compressed earth or sand is a good alternative. A dry riverbed is a great option but be wary of the possibility of flash flooding, and be vigilant with river stones as these can contain pockets of water and may explode in the heat of a fire!

Fire in snow or wet situations

If you're preparing the ground for a fire in snow or wet conditions, build a foundation of seasoned logs or sticks of roughly equal diameter across the platform, thus creating a dry and relatively warm 'floor' that will protect your efforts from any moisture beneath. The deadwood floor will become fuel at the heart of your fire and the gaps between the logs help draw air into the fire, feeding the combustion process.

Fire for warmth, fire for food

Before you begin you should think about what you want to achieve. Is the fire just for warmth or are you going to be cooking on it? If so, what are you cooking?

If you're planning on a quick meal and just need a fire for boiling or frying, make a small fire. You might want to support various cooking pots – perhaps a billy, griddle and frying pan. In this case, you'll want a low fire that's easy to control. Just using softwood might be the best tactic as it burns quickly and so is good for a fast fry.

The saying from an unknown Australian swagman, 'the bigger the fire, the bigger the fool' springs to mind when you see people creating huge bonfires just to boil up a billy.

BUILDING THE CAMPFIRE

There are many ways to build a campfire (or fire lay) and different styles can be used depending on the campfire's intended use. Some styles of fire lay are best suited to cooking, others to maximising heat or longevity. The success of any style of fire will be dependent on a combination of three essential elements: fuel, oxygen and ignition.

One of the most overlooked elements is the composition of the fire bed, which will need to be built in order to draw in the air (your oxygen component), up and through the construction. This is what will ensure a successful burn.

Once you've prepared the area for the fire, ensure that it's dry and protected from the wind. Lay out your fuel bundles outside of the fire pit area but close by. Start with a handful of tinder of your choice and lay down a couple of handfuls of the thinnest kindling that you have. Using a match or other fire-making device, light the tinder in the heart of the kindling bundle. As long as the material is dry and there's plenty of oxygen between the sticks, you should quickly have decent-sized flames. Add a handful of bigger fuel in a crisscross pattern. Don't add fuel unless the height of the flames is taller than the fuel, as you run the risk of suffocating the fire.

Keep building the fire, adding larger pieces of kindling, and then logs. Once the fire is blazing, you're in business. You can start boiling using pots, or wait a while for coals to appear for grilling or slow cooking. If you're not cooking, you can begin adding bigger fuel logs for a warming campfire.

Teepee fire lay

The teepee (or tipi) fire lay is an excellent choice for quickly starting a blazing hot campfire that will keep you toasty warm, or for quickly boiling a billy.

Start with a couple of handfuls (or more) of tinder and then lean a circle of thin kindling around the tinder. Continue the process with longer and larger pieces of kindling that are set slightly into the ground and lean into each other to provide a support structure for the rest of your fuel wood.

A teepee fire lay should have plenty of room between the different layers of kindling and fuel wood. The fire is directed up through the centre of the lay.

Log cabin fire lay

Also known as a funeral pyre, a log cabin fire lay is a good starting point for beginners. It's also great for cooking as the solid construction can support cookware.

Start by taking two long pieces of kindling and lay them parallel about 35cm (14in) apart. Then take another couple of similar-sized sticks and lay them perpendicular from each end on top of the original sticks. Within this square set-up add a couple of handfuls of tinder and some smaller kindling. Continue to build the log cabin by laying pieces of kindling in a crisscross pattern until you have five or six layers of fuel.

Pyramid fire lay

Also known as a top lighter, upside-down or platform fire, a pyramid fire lay is similar to the log cabin. However, the fire burns from the top downward. It's a good choice for cooking and for a long-lasting fire.

Start by taking two fuel logs of similar size and length (about an arm's width) and lay them parallel to each other on the ground, about 35cm (14in) apart. Add a layer of smaller logs about 10cm (2–3in) apart perpendicular to the base logs. Add three or four more layers in a crisscross pattern, with each layer using smaller and smaller logs until the top layer is pencil-sized kindling. Set a couple of handfuls of tinder on top of the fire lay.

Lean-to fire lay

While the lean-to is not the best fire for cooking on, it's an excellent fire for windy conditions and will provide great heat and light.

Start by taking a large hardwood log that your fire lay will lean against, and that will also provide protection from any wind which might interfere with your fire. Put some tinder next to the log and lean small pieces of kindling over the tinder pile. Add larger pieces of kindling against the log, being mindful to leave enough room to allow air to flow through the fire lay.

Campfire safety

'Fire makes a good servant but a cruel master.'
– proverb

Creating a fire is not without risk and should never be taken lightly. Vast bush and forest fires are now commonplace in the United States, Australia and other parts of the world. Most of these out-of-control fires are man-made and many are started by accident (unfortunately some are started deliberately). Don't be the person who starts one of these fires. Steps needs to be taken to prevent starting an uncontrolled fire, but in the event of an emergency situation you also need to know what to do.

Campfire precautions

- Before you leave for a trip, particularly in the back-country, research what restrictions are in place with the appropriate authorities (park or forestry management services, Bureau of Land Management, and so on). Remember that you may need a permit.
- Find out if there are existing facilities for campfires where you plan to camp.
- Check the weather before leaving. If it's the height of summer you can probably expect some sort of fire guidelines or even a fire ban.
- If you're building a fire lay yourself, follow the instructions laid out in the previous section, ensuring the appropriate clearance from any natural fuel or vegetation.

- Don't light or maintain a campfire on dry and windy days.
- Don't stack seasoned wood next to your fire.
- Never light a fire near a standing tree or stump.
- Keep your fire controlled and just big enough for your needs (warmth, cooking).
- Have a bucket or large container of water on hand.
- Never use flammable liquid or fuel on a fire (petrol, kerosene or diesel).
- Never leave a fire burning unattended.
- Don't burn dangerous or flammable items, like aerosol cans.
- Never put glass, tins, synthetics or plastics in your campfire.
- Don't let intoxicated people anywhere near a campfire.
- Supervise kids and pets at all times when near a fire.

Extinguishing a fire
- Allow the fire to burn down to ashes, if possible.
- Extinguish a fire thoroughly after use by dousing it with water, continually breaking and spreading the embers apart.
- Make sure the heart of the fire is cool to touch before leaving.
- Don't bury a fire in earth or sand unless you know it is completely extinguished.
- Adopt a Leave No Trace mindset (see p. 22).

WILDFIRE EMERGENCY

Whether driven by climate change, drought or increased natural fuel loads (for example, build-up of dry vegetation), there's no doubt that in some countries wildfires (or bushfires, as they are known in Australia) are increasing in number and intensity. In some places fire seasons are extending from spring through to early autumn. As this is high season for campers and hikers, it makes sense to prepare for an emergency. Check the various resources online and make sure you're aware of the risks before you go.

CAMPFIRE COOKERY

Even if you're not cooking a fancy cut of meat on hardwood charcoal and just some two-minute noodles, it's almost always a pleasure to eat camp cookery. Is it because of the exertion from the day's activity? The fresh air and magnificent view? The proximity to our natural environment?

Whatever the reason, being out in nature with simple fresh food has resulted in some of the best meals I've ever had. Freshly caught yellowfin tuna off the coast of New Zealand's North Island, thinly sliced sashimi-style on the side of a boat with plenty of soy sauce and wasabi, or a huge steak flash-grilled on a campfire after an epic 'lost-in-the-bush' 4WD death-defying misadventure in the Victorian High Country, careering down muddy valley tracks and over rocky escarpments (at best we thought we would be walking back to camp, if we were lucky!). It's a fact that campfire food beats a Michelin-quality restaurant every time!

Everyone loves a barbecue

When cooking on a wood-fuelled campfire, there's surely a primal instinct at work that connects us to our ancestral hunter-gatherer past. There's the ritual of building and tending to the fire itself. Then there's the chaotic slumber of the fire as the logs begin to carbonise. And finally there's the combusting wood which releases gasses and smoky impurities that impart the wood's unique character on your meal, giving you a real sense of place.

Around the world, and across almost all cultures, there's a reverence for cooking over a fire – Kobe Wagyu beef cooked yakiniku-style in Japan, the famous asado steaks cooked on a parrilla in Argentina, hawker-style chicken grilled on the streets in Bangkok, and chargrilled lamb on an ocakbasi grill in Turkey. The smell of char-cooked meat can induce an instinctive response, drawing people in.

A skill for all

In our modern era, cooking involves precision stoves with rotary knobs and thermostats controlled via a digital dashboard. Some smart stoves even connect to the internet and provide step-by-step recipe guidance from 'prep to plate'! Despite this, there's a keen interest in going back-to-basics and consequently we're seeing renewed interest in woodfire cookery. Camping is an excellent opportunity to develop this underused and ancient skill.

Cooking over a fire demands concentration in order to respond to the ever-changing conditions. Intuitiveness, spontaneity (and often luck) are key to getting a masterly result. Like any task worth doing, the right preparation and the right tools will help you succeed.

What to take

There's a whole section in this book dedicated to what to take on a camping trip and the kitchen is a major part of this (see p. 51). Naturally, there are major differences between what you would pack for a solo back-country hiking trip and a group or family camping trip with vehicles. For this section, we're going to assume that you're car camping. Although the mantra 'best kit for least weight and bulk' should always apply, I still recommend investing in certain items, like cast-iron cooking gear that goes against this motto but is the best equipment for the job.

Essential kit

You should be able to pack everything listed into a single tub. You can do a lot with one Dutch oven (shallow fry, boil water, use for washing-up) and some utensils.

But for a substantial kitchen kit this is what I would recommend:

1. chef's knife

2. paring knife

3. pocket knife or Leatherman

4. diamond sharpener

5. chopping board (two if possible – nested or a folding bamboo board are good options)

6. large serving spoon

7. stainless steel slotted spoon

8. long-handled barbecue tongs

9. long-handled barbecue spatula (a great improvisation is using a paint/putty scraper!)

10. long-handled barbecue fork

11. 22cm (9in) skillet

12. 30cm (12in) skillet

13. 25–30cm (10–12in) Dutch oven (good size for a leg of lamb and roast vegetables)

14. 3L (3qt) cooking pot

15. 5L (5qt) cooking pot

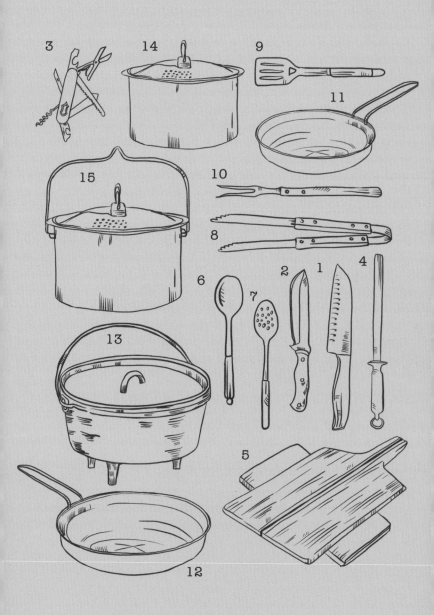

Other equipment

There are many ways to cook on an open fire. At the most basic end, all you really need is a green hardwood stick that you can use to hold food above the heat in order to crisp or roast it. But for most dishes – like stews, casseroles and fry-ups, or larger cuts of meat – you'll need to invest in some cooking equipment, utensils and tools to manage open-fire cooking.

Fireproof mitts or gloves

If you've spent any time cooking on an open fire you'll know that it's easy to burn yourself. A pair of fireproof mitts or gloves are essential for safe campfire cooking. Welding gloves are made to withstand extreme temperatures. They're inexpensive and available at most hardware stores.

Charcoal chimney starter

This is perhaps the quickest way to get hot coals ready for your fire pit. You can also use chimney starters to quickly top up your fire later on when it starts to lose heat. There are some chimneys that are designed for camping that foldaway flat.

Shovel

The folding variety is fine. You'll use a shovel for digging a fire pit and moving hot coals around, and also for camp chores and digging your vehicle out of sand traps.

Tripod

A tripod is a portable metal three-legged stand that's used to suspend pots and ovens over your fire from a hanging chain. Generally tripods are extendable, allowing you to control the heat by adjusting the height of the pot from the fire. They're perfect for boiling, braising or roasting with your pot or oven, and there's still room to use the fire beneath for cooking with another vessel, like a skillet.

Lid lifter

A lid lifter is a long cast-iron or stainless steel tool for hooking under and removing lids from pots or Dutch oven lids, or for retrieving bail-handle pots from the campfire.

Trivets

These are plate-shaped pieces of metal with vents that raise your food off the bottom of the oven, preventing it from burning and improving heat distribution.

Grill, grate, gridiron, griddle plates

A thick metal grill that supports your food at the right distance from the coal bed is a great way to cook on a campfire. Having a stable, flat surface is handy for pots, pans and kettles. You can adjust the height of the grill or move the coals into different layers beneath the grill to control the heat.

Cast-iron gridirons are heavy-duty metal grates with parallel bars that will heat up to extreme temperatures, giving your steaks, burgers and vegetables those pleasing chargrilled stripes.

Griddle plates are great for cooking smaller pieces of meat (rashers, chops, chicken) or vegetables without them falling through into the fire.

Skewers

I find that the sturdy stainless steel skewers with wooden handles that are made for shish kebabs are a very useful cooking tool for camping. They're generally inexpensive and are a simple (and fun) way of cooking meat and vegetables. Look for the traditional square skewer that's at least 40cm (16in) long.

Heavy duty portable camping spit roaster

Slowly cooking a joint of meat over an open fire is, for some, the height of primitive camp cooking and the next level in camp culinary achievement. A spit roaster (rotisserie) is the solution. It's essentially a long solid rod that skewers through a large joint of meat (or several joints) while being cooked over an open fire or metal fire pit. Using a portable spit roaster – or better yet, a spit you've fashioned from a green hardwood branch – is a sure-fire way to impress your fellow campers.

The variety of products available are endless. I've been coveting a spit roaster designed by a friend that's the perfect size for a leg of lamb or a chicken, with a rotisserie powered by a chargeable battery that packs down to less than 2kg (4lbs). The result is sublime.

Spit roasters designed for campers are either powered off 12V or have hand-cranked wind-up rotisseries. The slowly turning meat will self-baste, resulting in a sweetly charred, succulent roast that's full of flavour. Meanwhile, you can kick back and watch the show with a favourite beverage in hand.

Fuel

Bought wood

If you're unable to forage for wood locally you can always bring some with you. The same principles apply – softwood for kindling and hardwood for fuel logs. For the best results, make sure you're buying from a reputable source (not low-quality wood from your local gas station). You want wood that's properly seasoned and not going to let you down. The trick to creating a great flavour with wood-burning cooking is to reduce your fire down to smouldering coals.

Charcoal

Wood charcoal is produced by heating hardwood in a kiln devoid of oxygen (a process called 'pyrolysis') which results in carbonised wood with the volatile compounds (water, hydrogen, methane plus other tars and oils) removed.

If you're unable to forage or process wood at your campsite, charcoal is an economical fuel to bring on a trip. When compared to wood weight for weight, charcoal burns efficiently. It burns longer and gives out much more heat with very little smoke.

There are two main types of charcoal, lump charcoal and briquettes. Lump charcoal is charcoal in its purest form, whereas briquettes are processed charcoal with various additives and binding agents that can be quite toxic. I recommend using lump charcoal. There are numerous manufacturers who use various types of hardwood, including some that produce 'flavoured' smoke (cherry, apple and so on). Like most products, lump charcoal can vary in quality. Look for lump charcoal that has a high-temperature rating, long burn time and large ash production.

Another advantage of charcoal is that generally you can get a more consistent result. You can cook at specific temperatures, which is useful for less-forgiving dishes, like baked goods.

Building your fire pit

Construct a fire lay at one end of the fire pit, covering about a third of the length of the fire pit. Building a second, and even a third, fire with kindling tipis is a great way to get your cooking fire producing coal quickly.

After your fire has burnt for about half an hour, the flames will start reducing, logs will begin to break apart and produce red-hot coals, and after a while these coals will be layered with white ash. This is the optimum fuel for frying and grilling.

Using a shovel or tongs, you can move some of the hot coals to the other end of the fire pit. This will become your cooking fire. You'll need to keep stoking the fire's heat with fresh fuel as this will keep producing more hot coals for your cooking fire. The idea is to move the coals to create a bed of even heat.

Having a larger green log or rock at the back of your fire lay will reflect heat back into the cooking area. If you have time you can build a wall of horizontal green wood logs supported by vertical logs that have been driven into the ground. Favoured by bushcrafters, this type of construction, known as a reflector fire, increases the efficiency of your campfire and, if positioned correctly, acts as a windbreak.

Cooking

You now have the option of either cooking directly on the coals if you have a grill or tripod with legs, or you could use two green logs (or rocks) that are a similar size and thickness, placed either side of your bed of coals. This can support your Dutch oven, pot or skillets, giving you some extra control over the heat and coals.

You may want to have various cooking fires with support at different heights and fuels burning at different levels of heat for different cooking methods. For instance, a softwood high-flame fire for quick boiling, a low flame for braising meat, red-hot coals for grilling and searing, and older embers and ashes for vegetables.

Frying and searing

Frying and searing on a campfire with cast-iron will elevate you to a new level of culinary experience. Ever wondered why your home-cooked steak doesn't usually look the part? Why there's insipid fat and no deep dark browning? It's because home gas (or worse, electric) hobs will usually never get hot enough to sear your meat like a professional kitchen or real fire will.

Once you have enough blazing hot coals, preheat your skillet next to the fire so that the heat is more evenly distributed. This reduces the likelihood of burning food.

You can judge how hot your coals are by placing your hand above the coal bed with your palm facing downwards. The number of seconds that it's comfortable for indicates the level of heat: 1–2 is high, 3–4 is medium–high, 4–6 is medium, 6–8 is medium–low, and 8–12 is low.

For the best outcome use tallow instead of olive oil as it can handle the heat better. Get it almost to smoking point before adding your room-temperature, well-seasoned, dry-rubbed steak. Depending on the size of your steak, it should be seared at high heat for no more than a few minutes either side (unless it's still on the bone). Make sure that you rest it well before serving.

Watch out where you place your cast-iron pan after cooking, as it takes a long time before it's ready to be handled without protection. This also prevents the chance of thermal shock, which is caused by sudden extreme changes in temperature, like a red-hot cast-iron pan being doused with ice-cold water. Thermal shock can result in your cast-iron cracking.

Dirty steak

If you want to go completely primitive, a dirty steak is the go. Make sure you have a steak that's at least an inch (2.5cm) thick (T-bone or rib eye is sturdy enough for this) and seasoned with a little oil, garlic and a crust  of salt and pepper. Wait until you have red-hot coals with a layer of white ash, then place it directly on the coals for three minutes each side (five minutes for a two-inch or 5cm steak).

Once removed, brush off any debris and smother in butter. You're all set for sublimely charred meaty magic. This technique also works well with pork chops, but remove the fat first. Use a spice rub for lower-quality cuts.

Grilling

The main rule with grilling over a fire pit is to never cook directly over an open flame. This will quickly char and burn your food and it's a mistake people often make. You need patience to cook on a campfire and that means waiting until you have hot coals to work with.

The distance that your grill is set away from the fire and the heat of the coals (hot coals can burn up to 900°C or 1652°F!) will determine the cooking temperature. Usually you would aim to grill at least 10cm (4in) above the coal bed. It's ideal if you can adjust the grill to move up and down, thus adjusting the temperature.

Create a couple of different heat zones with different amounts of coals. Towards the back of the grill use larger layers (high heat) and grade down to a cool area, with little or no coals at the front of the grill. This is where you can 'retreat' your meat when flare-ups occur.

For fattier cuts, like chops or chicken thighs, cook them low and slow. I prefer to start off with a much gentler heat so that the fat of the meat starts to liquify first. This cooks the meat thoroughly before you finish it off by browning it over a higher heat. Be careful not to allow it to drip fat over the hot coals as the flare-ups can be violent and dangerous. You can minimise this by removing some of the fat from the meat prior to cooking and reducing the oil you use in marinades or when prepping your meat.

Cooking with fire is dynamic and things can change pretty quickly, with areas cooling at different rates depending on the fuel. So keep things moving and refresh your fuel with coals from your support fire.

Embers and ashes
The embers are simply the cooling coals breaking down into hot ashes. They offer the perfect heat for roasting vegetables. You can bury veggies – potatoes, sweet potatoes, butternut pumpkin (squash), Jerusalem artichokes, turnips, chestnuts, garlic and onions – in the hot ashes, or set them near hot coals, for an hour or so. When you retrieve your treasure from the fire, simply peel away the outer layer or slice the veggie in half and spoon out its soft centre. If you want to keep the skin of your veggie intact,

wrap it in foil before cooking or, better yet, in soaked banana or palm leaves.

To roast corn ears, soak them in water for an hour, then place them directly onto the hot coals. Cook for 30 minutes or so, turning a few times. You'll be rewarded with wonderfully charred husks and perfectly steamed corn. Just add butter, salt and pepper to achieve instant legend status.

If you want to get a little fancy, you can't beat hasselback potatoes. With their crispy outer layer and beautifully soft, creamy centre, they're a campfire favourite. Choose medium-sized roasting spuds. One by one, nestle the potatoes into the curve of a large wooden spoon. Using a sharp knife, slice downwards until your knife hits the edge of the spoon. Work the knife from one end of the potato to the other, spacing your slices about 0.5cm (0.125in) apart.

Meanwhile, heat some oil and butter in a pan along with thin slices of garlic. Brush your potatoes with the oil, butter and garlic mixture, then salt generously. Either wrap your spuds in foil or banana leaves, or arrange them in your favourite cookware – a Dutch oven is great for this. You can add grated cheese and chives at the end for extra points.

Dutch ovens

Although cast-iron Dutch ovens are a bulky and heavy item, after cooking with one you'll undoubtedly be a fan and will be ready to take your camp cooking to the next level. A Dutch oven's most basic use is boiling and simmering, just like any pot. But you can also use the Dutch oven in place of a skillet for sautéing vegetables or searing meats. They're perfect for cooking a breakfast fry-up with hash or corn fritters.

Where Dutch ovens really come into their own is their ability to function just like your oven at home. Because of the uniform heating, they're superb at baking, roasting and braising. A leg of lamb and roast potatoes is a sublime camping experience and total crowd-pleaser. A simple slow-cooked beef stew with plenty of red wine will have your camp mates salivating in no time. The great thing about Dutch ovens is that you can leave a meal cooking and get on with other tasks around camp.

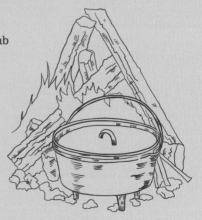

When cooking with a Dutch oven, temperature is controlled by placing the oven over a bed of coals and then covering the oven lid with more coals. You can easily adjust the temperature by removing or adding coals to the lid. Covering and then surrounding the oven with coals is the best way to bake, roast and braise with a Dutch oven.

For most recipes the ideal roasting temperature is around 180°C (350°F). But how many coals are needed to cook at this temperature? The answer depends on the fuel you're using and the size of your Dutch oven. The larger the oven, the more coals you'll need to maintain a consistent temperature. As a rule of thumb, use about a third of your fuel beneath the oven and two-thirds on top. Having fewer coals under the Dutch oven (where the food will be closer to the coals) helps prevent food from charring.

If you're using briquettes it's easier to apply some standardisation. You can use the chart on p. 154 as a guide to approximate temperatures based on how large your oven is and the amount of briquettes you have above and below the oven. A well-known formula for baking is to use just over twice the number of briquettes as the diameter of the oven, so for a 10-inch oven you would use 21 briquettes, with 14 on top and 7 below to achieve a temperature of 180°C (350°F).

You'll need to keep fresh hot coals on hand for any recipe with a cooking time longer than half an hour, so keep adding fuel to your original fire, or use a charcoal chimney starter to create more hot briquettes.

Although all of this is by no means accurate, it still gives you a good starting point. You can adjust the amount of fuel based on your own experience as you gain an understanding of the different fuel types, the characteristics of your own equipment and the effects of the environment. Practice makes perfect!

Dutch oven temperature/no. of briquettes guide

OVEN SIZE		160°C/ 325°F	175°C/ 350°F	190°C/ 375°F	205°C/ 400°F	220°C/ 425°F	235°C/ 450°F
8"	Top	10	11	11	12	13	14
	Bottom	5	5	6	6	6	6
10"	Top	13	14	16	17	18	19
	Bottom	6	7	7	8	9	10
12"	Top	16	17	18	19	21	22
	Bottom	7	8	9	10	10	11
14"	Top	20	21	22	24	25	26
	Bottom	10	11	12	12	13	14

Cleaning

I think it's best to clean as you go. This is supremely easy with cast-iron as you just add water to a cooled skillet or Dutch oven and bring it to the boil over the fire, scraping away the residue food and fat. Make sure you dispose of the residue carefully so that you don't have wild animals sniffing around all night! Once cleaned, you can reapply a little oil and thrust the skillet back into the fire for a quick seasoning. Then you're set for action the next day!

6

Things to do around camp

Hiking

'Walking is man's best medicine.'
– Hippocrates, date unknown

'Now shall I walk
Or shall I ride?
"Ride," Pleasure said;
"Walk," Joy replied.'
– William Henry Davies, 'The Best Friend', 1905

From a simple walk in the woods to a multi-week thru-hike,
walking in nature has a special attraction for us humans. No doubt
it has been hardwired into our DNA. Just like camping, cooking
with fire and stargazing, from an evolutionary perspective a
hike in the wilderness is a common part of human history. Our
earliest ancestors roamed vast expanses of wilderness at least
200,000 years ago.

I've been fortunate to experience some incredible hiking – in New
Zealand the Tongariro Alpine Crossing, Routeburn and Milford
Tracks, and Lake Waikaremoana are highlights. Internationally,
the well-trodden (but well worth it) Inca Trail in Peru, The Lycian

Way in Turkey and the Alps of Italy have been favourites. Here in Australia, the Larapinta Trail in the Northern Territory was a special experience. Probably the most remote hike I've done was climbing active volcanoes in Kamchatka – a peninsula in Far East Russia with over 160 volcanoes (and plenty of bears!).

While I have wonderful memories of these epic adventures, I also find great joy in simple walks closer to home. Our kids love these shorter walks too – racing ahead, hunting for bugs under tree bark, picking up sticks and spotting wildlife. Often just a 30-minute stroll among the trees is all you need to lift your mood.

Of late, much has been made of adopting a primitive lifestyle when it comes to nutrition and fasting, but we could also benefit from taking on primitive physical activities, like regular walking and hiking. From studying the remnants of hunter-gatherer people, researchers know that they walked at least 10km (6mi) a day on average. Contrast that with the average modern American who walks less than a third of that distance a day.

Surprisingly, given that anatomically the human body is primed for walking, it's an underrated form of holistic exercise. Plenty of studies link walking with not only improved physical health – reduced blood pressure, improved digestion, reduced inflammation – but also with improved mental health – heightened mood and clarity of thought. It can even reverse an ageing brain!

I – and many others – believe that walking (particularly solo) has a clear link to mindfulness meditation (*see* p. 220). Studies on walking as meditation show decreases in depression and stress. Other studies show that walking with intention can reduce cortisol in the blood, the body's primary stress-indicating hormone. In short, walking is good for you!

Walking has been celebrated by many of the world's historic great thinkers. Socrates, Charles Darwin, Henry David Thoreau, Friedrich Nietzsche, Immanuel Kant, John Muir and many others believed that walking in nature was a path to pure thought and creativity, uninhibited by distraction.

Hiking evokes the great journeys of early explorers – Lewis and Clark's crossing of America or Burke and Wills' ill-fated Australian expedition to find an inland sea that didn't exist. There's a certain thrill to be had from taking a backpack with minimal gear and food and tackling a trail, not knowing exactly where you'll camp for the night. There's always the potential for adventure.

It's unfortunate that many perceive hiking as some sort of adrenaline sport, conquering summits and collecting famous hikes like trophies. There can also be a certain amount of gear nerdery from certain parts of the community. While it's healthy to challenge yourself, and having equipment that aids your endeavour is important, for me hiking is simply an opportunity to witness nature at a human-friendly pace, perspective and scale. A way to experience the micro, as well as the macro, details of a landscape.

Moreover, unlike travelling in a vehicle or riding a bicycle, when you walk you're actively participating in the environment and have the ability to move yourself in any direction at any time, which elicits a certain sense of freedom.

Beyond the physical and psychological, walking, and in particular hiking, has a lot to offer the budding outdoors person. But before you head off into parts unknown, it pays to plan and prepare for a hike.

WHAT'S IN A NAME?

Backpacking (United States/Canada), tramping (New Zealand), rambling and hill walking (United Kingdom), and bushwalking (Australia) are all interchangeable terms associated with particular countries. They all signify walking in nature, normally on a trail or track, potentially overnight. They usually involve carrying extra clothing, food and, possibly, shelter. For ease I'll use the universal term 'hiking'.

The key thing to note is that although hiking may require planning, some basic navigation skills and fitness, no real technical knowledge is necessary to undertake a hike. The exception to this is trekking which may involve a more technical or arduous journey, requiring extra preparation and equipment. Trekking is usually associated with organised mountain or jungle hikes in groups with specially trained guides leading.

WHAT TO BRING

What you'll bring on a hike is dictated by the duration of the hike and the environment you'll encounter. Naturally, a day hike on a well-marked and frequently used track will require a different set of needs than a multi-day thru-hike across elevated terrain in winter where you'll require specialist gear that will need to perform, otherwise it could be life threatening.

Which gear to take hiking is a topic that is potentially limitless and, I think, can be a time-waster for marginal gains. Do you really need that ridiculously pricey jacket made from some super-duper space-age fabric? Good gear can be expensive, but in my opinion there is a price point threshold where there are only marginal performance benefits to be had. Do your research to find the best quality brand at a price you can afford.

There's a whole industry focused on innovating ultra-functional, lightweight and durable gear. Every conceivable piece of gear that you'll need is available in different materials and at different price points.

The best advice is do your research. Talk to staff in stores, read forums and think about how often you'll use items before spending up big on the latest must-have piece of clothing. Try not to get bogged down in the minutiae spouted by gear nerds. Just aim for the best gear at a price you can afford (or just borrow it from a friend who likes fancy stuff!).

Clothing

Clothing is something to get right and will make the biggest difference to your comfort levels. You should always pack for any eventuality.

Lots of thin layers, rather than one bulky one, is best as you can create the perfect amount of insulation needed while on the move. It's easier to add layers than take them off, so start with the least amount of clothing that's comfortable for the weather conditions.

Layers that are already wet from sweat or rain will take longer to soak into the next layer and can easily be removed. Also pack a second set of clothes that will remain dry. You want to at least sleep in dry underwear.

Synthetics and polyester fleeces are the best materials for hiking. Leave the cotton and wool at home – when it's wet it's heavy and hard to dry!

Footwear

Hiking boots should be as lightweight as possible, waterproof and have a breathable inner lining. You want footwear that will dry easily. I really like Vibram soles but a lot of hikers just use lightweight running shoes. Again it depends on the environment, the weather and your own preferences.

Backpacks

Having a backpack that fits your torso correctly is the key to comfortable travel by foot. Your torso length is the key measurement to determine what size pack will best suit you.

Backpacks can be either a fixed length or an adjustable length. The latter allows you to adjust the length of the backpack to fit your torso exactly, so weight is transferred from the shoulders to the hips, which is a more comfortable way to carry. Fixed-length backpacks tend to be much lighter but you'll need to find one that fits correctly.

Other than the adjustable suspension of your pack, you should consider the various strap systems, pack capacity, materials, construction, padding, zippers, pockets and other features. There's a whole world of backpacks out there.

The 10 essentials:
What to take hiking

There are plenty of checklists online (*see* www.homecamp.com.au/camping-checklist) but these 10 essentials are an excellent guide on what to pack for any outdoor adventure. They cover all the main categories so you can use them as a master checklist to make sure you have all the bases covered prior to setting off.

'The 10 essentials' is a now-iconic list that was first published in the 1930s by the Mountaineers Club and is well-known among the outdoors community. The original list was proposed as a response to two fundamental questions a mountaineer should ask before embarking on an expedition:

- Can you respond positively to an accident or emergency?
- Can you safely spend a night or more outside in an emergency?

The classic 10 essentials recommended are:

- map
- compass
- sunglasses and sunscreen
- extra clothing
- headlamp or flashlight
- first-aid supplies
- fire starter
- matches
- knife
- nutrition.

The list has been revised several times and is now known as the '10 essentials system', giving the list a more flexible and functional approach. To this day, it is still the go-to list that should form the basis of any kit you take when heading out into the wilderness, either by foot or in a vehicle. It's also an ideal emergency kit to have in your car at all times.

Even on a day hike, it's good practice to take at least a partial kit, as it trains you for preparedness.

The 10 essentials are a good guide for adventures big and small, but do your research. Always expect the best but prepare for the worst.

Here's how the 10 essentials system breaks down, along with some extra ideas I've added:

1. NAVIGATION

It's not only sensible but essential (especially in remote areas) to know where you are, where you intend to go and what the best route is.

Get into the habit of always taking a map and using a compass. Maps are fun to use and keep your senses attuned to the landscape and its features. Practise using a baseplate compass with a mirror. It doubles as a signalling device and a solar ignition if you find yourself without a lighter.

There are a variety of handheld satellite navigation devices available which are more robust than your phone and have extra battery life and better coverage in the back-country. This is a good addition to a map and compass, not a replacement.

If you're on a multi-day hike have a printed itinerary with dates and stops and send a digital copy to friends or family before you leave.

2. SUN PROTECTION

Sun protection is drummed into us from an early age here in Australia and as a result almost everyone is sun aware. A proper wide-brim hat, sunglasses, lip balm and sunscreen are essential in all hot climates as severe sunburn, heat stroke and dehydration are extremely dangerous.

3. HEADLAMP AND HIGH-POWERED TORCH (FLASHLIGHT)

If you do much overnight hiking you'll know that often there are very early starts and sometimes late arrivals due to unforeseen circumstances. Illumination is the key to finding your way, and each other, in the dark. A headlamp or torch (flashlight) is a must-have item for any emergency kit. A high lumen torch (flashlight) can double as a signalling device. Bring extra batteries.

4. FIRST-AID KIT AND INSECT REPELLENT

A comprehensive first-aid kit should be in every vehicle when heading into the wild. If you're hiking you should take an extra basic first-aid kit, including painkillers, Band-Aid, stretch tape and antibiotic ointment.

Keep your kit in a ziplock bag or dry pouch. In some countries (United States, Australia) you might want to consider taking extra precaution with a snake-bite kit.

5. KNIFE AND TOOLS

A Swiss Army knife or Leatherman is the perfect multitool to take on any outdoor trip. Combine this with a decent full-tang knife and you've covered a lot of bases. You can repair items, process wood for a fire or even make a shelter.

6. FIRE

A well-considered fire-starting kit that'll work in any eventuality is essential. A good kit will include waterproof matches and lighters and potentially a ferro rod or fire strike as a backup device. You should keep some tinder that is guaranteed to take a spark in your kit. Stow your kit in a sealed waterproof container or dry pouch.

7. INSULATION

Aside from access to water, insulation is probably the most essential lifesaver, especially in bad weather. What clothes you take will vary depending on the type of terrain and time of year. A change of underwear, beanie, socks and gloves are recommended.

Also consider:

- Hiking boots or running shoes are best. Some hikers take lightweight camp slip-ons that double as wading shoes. Also consider lightweight clogs, sandals, Crocs or neoprene socks with hard soles.
- Lightweight vest or jacket insulated with down or synthetic material.
- Synthetic base layers made from polypropylene and a fleece (avoid cotton).
- Long pair of synthetic hiking pants that can convert to shorts.
- Hard-shell raincoat with hood and rain pants made from a synthetic like Gore-Tex.
- Breathable synthetic underwear that will dry easily and draw moisture away. Synthetics don't tend to bunch up as much when you sweat, so reduce painful chafing.
- Two pairs of socks. Make sure you find fit-for-purpose merino wool or synthetic-mix socks with padding. They make a huge difference to comfort and prevent bunching and blisters. A synthetic mix will also dry quickly.
- Sleeping bag that is rated correctly for the season.
- Sleeping pad.
- Gloves, fleece beanie, trekking umbrella, cap.
- Waterproof bivvy or emergency bivvy.

8. SHELTER

Even if you're going on a day hike it's worth taking a lightweight emergency shelter, either an emergency bivvy (basically a thermal bag made of heat-reflective polythene) or a lightweight plastic poncho or tarp.

For longer trips you should research and invest in a lightweight tent, tarp or hammock set-up.

9. NUTRITION

The body needs about 700g to 1kg (1.5–2.2lb) of food a day. It makes sense to pack nutrition-dense food that provides the most energy for the least amount of weight.

It's tempting to pack sugar-heavy foods, but food that is rich in protein, complex carbohydrates and glucose releases more energy over prolonged periods of sustained activity. Carbohydrates are also the best fuel to keep warm and in cooler weather you can top up before bed for a warm night's sleep.

You want to pack foods that don't require much preparation. Dehydrated meats, jerky, cheese and fresh fruit, along with trail mix (dehydrated fruit and nuts), breakfast or protein bars, and chocolate are good options.

10. HYDRATION (EXTRA WATER)

Take a minimum of 2L (2qt), stored in either a couple of bottles or a bladder. Add a screw-on filter and a backup method of treating water, for example, a water purifier straw or chemical treatment.

Barring a life-threatening injury, staying warm and hydrated are the most important items on this list. Without them you could find yourself in a potentially life-threatening situation.

What else?

You should always aim to have a communications device with you. Either a phone with an extra battery or charging device, or satellite phone if you're going remote. We take a set of walkie talkies that the kids love and are handy if you're in a group walking at different speeds.

Emergency kit

Your emergency kits should contain a first-aid kit, fire kit and a Personal Locator Beacon (PLB). A simple emergency whistle is a small item that can be easily attached to your backpack and can save lives.

PROTECT WILDLIFE FROM YOUR FOOD

Have you ever been woken up at three in the morning by marauding wombats or rambunctious raccoons? I've even heard of encounters with hungry badgers in the United Kingdom! It pays to keep your food out of your tent and away from camp, preferably hanging from a tree. Rig up a dry bag with a length of paracord and winch it up a tree. If you're in bear country use a plastic canister that's bear-proof.

HYGIENE

There's no need to be feral when on a multi-day hike. Bring a lightweight camping towel made from ultra-absorbent material that dries quickly. Take thicker paper towels for toilet use as they'll perform better than toilet paper in humid conditions. Hand sanitiser is a must when camping and hiking. Change your underwear daily and wash and dry them as you go (remember the Leave No Trace principles – *see* p. 22).

DAY HIKING

Before jumping in and planning a multi-night hike across your nearest mountain range, it makes sense to start with shorter, achievable hikes that will allow you to evaluate your own fitness, gear and test other skills like navigation and map reading.

A short day hike is a good way to start. Choose a hike somewhere as close to where you live as possible, over minimal elevation that is graded 'easy' for beginners and lasts between 1 and 3 hours. A circuit that returns you to your starting point is a great choice. The beauty of a day hike is that you won't need to invest much in the way of specialist equipment. For example, depending on the terrain, you may be able to hike in lightweight running shoes, rather than expensive boots, and without a backpack.

Inspiration can come from many places. Instagram is a popular source and there are many specialist hiking apps. Word of mouth, guidebooks, national or state park authorities, outdoor retailers, hiking clubs and the many hiking forums are all excellent resources.

Day hikes are a good way to build fitness and strength, to identify potential physical weaknesses that may need attention and to get an understanding of your average hiking pace. This will all come in handy when planning future overnight hikes. Once you have a few under your belt, work your way up to longer hikes.

The next step would be to camp in an area with multiple day hikes close by, so you have a base camp to return to each day. You can often drive to the campsite that you'll use as your base camp which means you'll have more luxury and food on hand.

Before you go

Use a weather app to check the conditions before you set off and make sure you have plenty of daylight to complete the hike. If it's hot bring sun protection and if it's cool bring extra clothing. Whatever the weather, you should take a waterproof layer and a warm layer.

While hiking solo is enjoyable and can be meditative, a group hike is an excellent way to socialise with friends while feeling protected. If you're hiking solo make sure your destination is safe and that you let friends or family know where you intend to hike and what time you plan to return.

MULTI-DAY HIKES

After completing numerous day hikes you may want to tackle the greater challenge of a multi-day hike. Before choosing where and when you'll hike you need to honestly check in with your own capabilities to evaluate your skills and fitness level. This should be the first thing that informs your planning.

Ask yourself about your motivations and goals. Are you looking for a personal challenge or interested in meeting new people? Hiking can be a highly social pastime, with clubs and meet-ups dedicated to connecting like-minded people. Or maybe you're more inclined to seek out solitude in the wilderness. Perhaps you have an interest in nature photography, or the history of a particular area.

You want to look for the right level of challenge that won't override your enjoyment of the hike (you can move on to tougher stuff later). Whatever your motivations, you should think this through before committing to your first overnight hike and the level of challenge will help you narrow down the options.

It's easier to hike in a dry and warm season at first. Choose somewhere popular and take the path well-trodden, where there are others who can lend a hand if required.

Planning

Once you have settled on a destination for a multi-day hike you should begin to gather as much information about the hike as possible. Check out guide books or look for a good online resource or one of the many apps (alltrails.com is great!).

I find buying a physical topographic map of the hike and surrounds really helps you to familiarise yourself with the terrain you'll encounter and the location of the trailhead (the point at which the trail begins). You can explore potential routes, plot elevation and distances, camping options and water resources along the way.

Check out the seasonal weather data and trip reports from other hikers so you can compile more information. Call the local rangers' department and ask their opinion on the route and conditions you might expect. Sometimes the route you want to take might be closed because of maintenance or any number of other reasons. They will usually give you personal advice about the best access points, campsites and facilities available, and they should be able to tell you about any potential hazards along the route, for example, rockslides, fallen trees and detours. Ask about the wildlife you'll encounter and find out if you need a permit or booking with the park first.

Itinerary

Nerd alert! I find it really helpful to capture all this information along with links in a spreadsheet so you can easily build an itinerary.

Once you have a broad outline of the target route, you can start planning in more detail. Research how long it will take you to and from the trailhead and add this to your itinerary. Estimate the time and distances for each section of the hike based on your own pace and crosscheck this estimation with online reviews, forums or park information. Plot your camping spots near water sources and notable landmarks along your chosen route. Add in any side trips. Note any evacuation advice that you can find.

Plan out each meal and your daily water requirements. It may help to add the ingredients to your spreadsheet and calculate your total food and water consumption. Add in extra time and provisions.

Even if you're using physical topographic maps you can also use an app like Maps.me to download a map of the area that will still work offline.

Share the load

I think it's safer and more enjoyable to go on a multi-day hike with at least one other person. You can share the planning, get excited about the trip and also lower your backpack load by sharing a tent, cooking gear, food and so on. Having a hiking buddy also means that you'll have a helping hand should you come across any difficulties.

Packing and final preparations

How you pack your backpack can have an impact on your journey and your comfort. Being organised is key and, much like packing your car for car camping, you should gather all your gear together in one place, categorise everything and pack the gear you're least likely to use first into the bottom of your pack. Try to pack heavier items deeper to make sure your pack is well-balanced.

Rolling up clothing saves space, and using compression sacks, packing cubes and dry bags is a good way to reduce bulk. I use several different sack sizes for different categories of gear – clothes, cooking items, tech, emergency kit, miscellaneous.

It makes sense to have clothing layers, a jacket and toiletries towards the top. Side pockets, slings and belt pockets are good places to keep your navigation gear, snacks, water, sunscreen, sunglasses, car keys and wallet.

Most backpacks will have some webbing loops or MOLLE systems (that's Modular Lightweight Load-carrying Equipment!). These are very useful for strapping on longer items – for example, tent poles or a sleeping pad – using a webbing strap or carabiner.

When you're finished, weigh your packed backpack. It shouldn't exceed more than about a third of your body weight, but will ideally be around a quarter.

Let someone know

Discuss your plan with a friend or family member who is not going on the trip. Send them your itinerary and make sure it includes your expected return date and time, and contact information for the authorities with instructions of what to do if you don't contact your family member by a pre-agreed time. Many national parks will allow you to call ahead or register your hike online.

Before you head off, print your trip itinerary and notes. Keep it with your maps in a waterproof map case. Make final equipment checks (stove fuel, spare batteries) and check the weather forecast one last time before heading off on your adventure.

NAVIGATION

If you're camping at established campsites or at your local holiday park, the most taxing navigation skill you'll need is finding the shower block at night! But the more you head out into the wilderness to hike, hunt, 4WD or camp, the more you'll want to explore off the beaten track. Even if you're doing little more than a short walk on a well-marked track, you should consider how to safely navigate the route.

A friend of mine was once camping solo in the Victorian highlands of Australia in a remote area, hours away from the main road. After making camp and sleeping the night, he set off the next morning on foot in search of firewood and took his camera to shoot some photos along the way. Within a short time he became so absorbed in taking photos that he completely forgot to gauge where he was going. Eventually he realised that he was hopelessly lost.

Minutes stretched into hours and he still couldn't find his way back to his camp and vehicle. This guy is a fairly competent camper but walking through a wooded area of an extensive wilderness region with no GPS or map to guide you can be disorientating for anyone. That night he had to sleep rough. The next day he tried to find his camp again and it was only through sheer luck that he eventually stumbled across an infrequently used fire access track that led to his campsite and vehicle.

The experience shook him up and he recognised that he'd been overly confident and incredibly unprepared. So don't be that guy!

Reliance on GPS

Each year we hear horror stories of trusting folk who have been misdirected by their smartphone mapping system and sent in the wrong direction, resulting in them being seriously lost. It highlights our reliance on imperfect technology. Unfortunately, some situations end in a tragedy. In many circumstances, disaster could have been averted with some basic navigation skills and enough awareness to challenge the directions offered by the GPS.

GPS is *the* digital clock by which all digital communications are synchronised. It's used by just about anything that requires precise mathematical calculations of location in time and space. It fixes your position using converging location data that it receives from multiple satellites. GPS systems and smartphones are reliant on a power source, the correct mapping and geospatial data and satellite coverage to work – all of which are by no means guaranteed when on a remote back-country adventure.

Alongside this, applications like Google Maps are making traditional map-reading skills almost obsolete. There's now concern within the scientific community that we aren't exercising the crucial areas of our brain that create spatial maps and this, in turn, is leading to some sort of atrophy. There are even links being made to Alzheimer's.

Types of navigation

Being able to construct cognitive maps in the mind was unquestionably a skill that our ancestors had. Until paper maps were widely used, most people would have travelled across the country by remembering various landmarks, and this knowledge would have been passed on by word of mouth.

Indigenous peoples of Australia used an elaborate system called 'songlines' to record and transmit maps and routes across vast distances of land. By singing the songs in the appropriate sequence, a knowledgeable person could reveal the embedded terrain features, waterholes and other useful information, unravelling a detailed map of the country ahead.

Just like our ancestors, using your eyes and a good memory of the terrain features you've crossed is a fine way to navigate. For fun, if you have a pen and paper, you could simply draw your own map as you walk to remind you of the terrain you've covered! But if you're doing any sort of serious hiking or back-country exploration you should learn how to use a map and compass.

Navigation with a map and compass
Navigating with a map and compass is a skill that anyone can learn. Finding your way using these tools is fun and (with a bit of experience) it's a reasonably fail-safe way of getting from A to B.

Paper maps rarely display incorrect information and don't require batteries. Likewise, compasses are simple and reliable and fairly indestructible. These two devices together are a time-tested, assured method of keeping you on the right track.

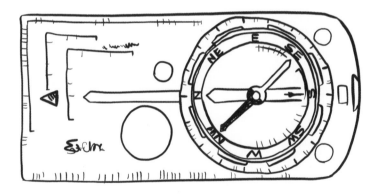

Compasses

A compass is an instrument used to keep you pointed in an accurate direction, or to take a 'bearing' between points, measured in units of degrees from north. In theory, this allows you to move across the terrain in a straight line from point to point. In practice, there's hardly ever a straight-line path in the back-country!

Compasses become important in inclement weather when you lose the ability to navigate by the sun (obscured by clouds or fog) and you only have the immediate features of the terrain and a map to work with.

Magnetic compass

A magnetic compass is an instrument that's been in use by navigators, explorers and everyday travellers for over 1000 years. It generally consists of some sort of device in a protective case (or housing) that displays the cardinal and intermediate directions in a circle from north to east, south, west, then back to north again. Additionally, there will usually be an indication of bearings marked in degrees. For example, north would be represented by the bearing 0°, east by 90°, south by 180°, and west by 270°.

Compass bearings are simply the angle measured in degrees relative to north and are always measured in a clockwise direction. Some compasses will have a full 360° marked, and others will be marked in increments (or gradations) of 20°.

A magnetic needle is attached to a central swivel that's been magnetised to always point towards magnetic north. So by using this fixed direction we can determine the route we want to take or are already travelling in. Compasses can also be used to fix your position on a map.

Baseplate compass

Most modern map compasses designed for the outdoors person are small, handheld devices with a flat transparent underside, called a baseplate, that can be laid flat onto a map. These are the best type of compass or map reading and setting a course while on the move.

A baseplate compass (also sometimes called an orienteering or protractor compass) consists of a durable plastic housing filled with a liquid, like oil, that keeps the compass needle action working smoothly. This type of compass will have an outer rotating dial (called a bezel or graduated dial) which can be used to set your bearing. The baseplate sides will have a straight edge, sometimes called a baseline, with a ruler and various scales for calculating distances and plotting coordinates.

Knowing your north and adjusting for declination

Unfortunately for the compass operator, there's a difference between true north (or geodetic north), which is the exact location of the North Pole, and magnetic north, which is governed by the Earth's magnetic field which fluctuates over time and is always relative to the observer's current position. The difference between true north and magnetic north is measured in degrees and this is known as 'declination'.

As the Earth changes position over time so does the declination. This is why old maps are often out-of-date and inaccurate for navigation. Some of the Earth's regions have a large declination. For example, New Zealand currently has a difference between 18–26°, while most of Europe is currently only 1–4°.

To get an accurate reading with your compass, you should allow for this difference and know the declination for the area you're visiting. Most maps will tell you what adjustment you need to make, but if not you can research online before you leave.

The third and final north is grid north. This is shown at the top of all topological maps and the direction of the vertical grid lines from the bottom of the map to the top.

Orient yourself and your map:

1. Lay your compass down flat on top of the map with the direction of travel (DOT) arrow pointing toward the top of the map (grid north) furthest away from you.

2. Adjust the baseplate until the straight edge (or baseline) is parallel with the left or right edge of your map, while keeping the DOT pointing toward the top of the map.

3. Rotate the bezel until the N (north) is perfectly aligned with the DOT and top of your map.

4. Hold both map and compass steady horizontally, rotate your body until the end of the magnetic needle is within the outline of the orienting arrow.

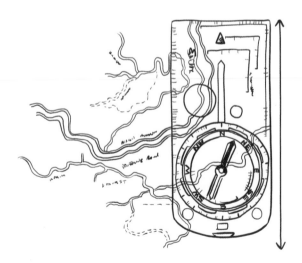

You're now ready to read your map. If you're in an open or elevated position you should be able to look around in any direction and recognise terrain features and landmarks that appear on the map. You can now rotate the map until the features on the map and the features in the terrain are in their correct relative position to your body and the direction you intend to travel.

The next step is to find the bearing you'll use to travel to your destination.

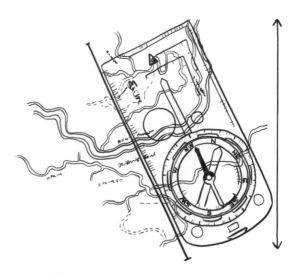

Take a bearing from your map:

1. Lay your map down flat with the top of the map (grid north) furthest away from you. Mark your position (A), then the position you want to get to (B).

2. Using your baseplate flat edge (or baseline), align the edge in a straight line from A to B with the direction of travel (DOT) arrow pointing in the direction you want to go (B).

3. Keep your compass baseplate in the initial position, rotate the bezel until the N (north) on the bezel and the orienteering arrow are pointing to the top of your map (grid north). The orienteering lines should also be aligned with the grid lines that point north on your map.

4. Remove the compass from the map and use your index line to take a bearing. You can now adjust your compass for declination (record this bearing).

5. Hold your compass in front of you horizontally with the DOT arrow pointing straight ahead and away from you, then slowly turn yourself and the compass until the red end of the needle is within the orienting arrow.

6. Congratulations, you've taken your first bearing! Now look for a static feature or landmark in the direction you intend to travel and set a course for it.

7. Now it's just a case of ensuring the magnetic needle is within the orienting arrow and the DOT arrow is pointing in the direction that you intend to travel.

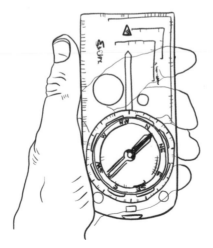

Using bearing to find where you are on a map

From time to time you'll want to know your exact position on a
map so that you can, for instance, judge how far you are along
a trail. You can use a method known as 'triangulation' to find your
exact position.

1. Study two visible terrain features or landmarks
   (for example, a hill and creek) that you can see
   from your current position.

2. Determine where they are on your map and mark
   them as Location 1 (L1) and Location 2 (L2).

3. Hold the compass out in front of you and point the
   DOT arrow toward L1.

4. Rotate the bezel until the magnetised needle is
   inside the orienting arrow.

5. Take your first bearing at the index line.

6. Place the compass back on your map with the
   baseplate corner touching L1.

7. Pivot the compass around on L1 until the orienting
   arrow and lines line up with the meridian lines on
   your map.

8. Using the baseline on the baseplate, draw a line
   from L1 across your map in the direction that you
   think you are in in relation to L1.

9. Repeat the same process for L2. The two lines
   should intersect and this is your position.

Moving through the landscape

If you're in an open landscape with well-marked tracks and clear weather, there's not much call for continuously checking your bearing with a compass. Just make sure that the map is correctly oriented with your surroundings and grid north is always facing magnetic north. It's good to practise to not only mark your route on a map but also the landmarks you'll use to check your progress.

You can periodically stop to identify recognisable landmarks on your map and in your line of sight. These are called 'steering marks' and are a useful aid in checking your direction without constantly referring to your compass and map.

It may be that the terrain feature or landmark – a hill or ridge, perhaps – will need to be circumnavigated. That's okay, you can take a reading with your map and compass after you've moved around the object and need to change direction back towards your destination.

Aiming off

Another way to solve this is to try 'aiming off'. This is simply aiming for another prominent landmark or landscape feature that is on either side of your target but has easier access. Once you arrive at the feature, it should be easy enough to turn left or right to reach your target destination.

Handrail

Another tip is to look for a recognisable linear feature on your map that's easily identifiable in the landscape and also happens to be in the direction you want to go, for example, a ridgeline, coastline or fence. This feature is called a 'handrail' and by traversing it, or simply using it as a line-of-sight guide, you can move quickly and confidently towards your destination.

In addition, use the sun's position to determine the direction you want to travel in (see p. 190) and the changes in direction you've made. You should be able to note the orientation of the features you're passing (for example, large rock facing east).

As your journey progresses you should consciously memorise significant landmarks that you've passed during your outbound journey, like trees, boulders and hillocks. Use frequent stops to look back and familiarise yourself with the terrain you've already passed and the landmarks you've met from the opposite angle. This will come in handy on the return journey when you can mentally tick off the features of the same terrain in reverse order as you go.

Getting out into nature, consciously studying the terrain and paying attention, tunes you into your surroundings like never before. The more you can do this without the aid of a map and compass, the more you're developing the underutilised and ancient skill of building spatial maps in the mind.

Reading maps and the terrain

Good maps are fairly easy to find, are usually accurate, don't require power and can save lives. Many countries have government agencies responsible for mapping, including the Ordnance Survey (United Kingdom), U.S. Geological Survey (USGS, United States) and Geoscience Australia. Often they provide their geospatial and mapping data to third parties – like National Geographic in the United States – who will incorporate other datasets into a single specialist map for a particular use, like trail hiking.

A bushwalking or hiking map is likely to be at a different scale and will highlight different features than a road map which is used for driving from city to city. For most outdoor exploration you'll be looking for a specialist topographic map (or topo map) which will give you information about the shape, elevation and characteristics of the terrain you're travelling through. Ideally, it will mark trails, campsites, lookouts and other natural features that will be of interest to the hiker or camper.

1. Contours

One major advantage of a topographic map is that it will show contours, which is a way of judging elevation in terms of the steepness or gentleness of a slope.

The gap between contours on a topographic map is known as a contour interval (CI) and this indicates the differences in elevation. On most hiking maps the elevation difference between consecutive contours will be marked in the legend, usually at intervals of 5, 10 or 20m (16, 32 or 65ft). The contours are drawn as reddish-brown lines – sometimes spread out, and sometimes closer together. The closer the contours are the steeper the elevation. This is powerful because it allows you to visualise the terrain as a three-dimensional landscape, thus aiding your route planning and helping you avoid any potential hazards or obstructions.

If you study a topographic map you'll notice that every fifth contour line is slightly bolder and will have a number labelled within the line. This is the elevation of that contour. As you go uphill this number will increase, and as you go downhill it will reduce. If you look at the next bold contour line and calculate the difference between them, then divide by five, this will give you the difference in elevation between contours.

Concentric lines that end in a small circle usually indicate a summit. Occasionally you may see elevations decrease and end in a circular contour with some tick lines – this is a basin or depression.

2. Scales

Map scales are a way of reducing distances in the real world into a representation in two dimensions. Scales are expressed as a

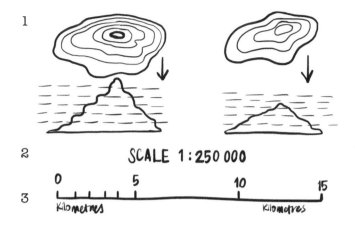

1

2 SCALE 1:250 000

3
0   5   10   15
Kilometres   Kilometres

ratio. For example, a 1:25000 scale means for every 1cm on the map, in the real world there's 25,000cm or 0.25km. So at this scale 4cm will equal 1km in the real world.

The lower the second number, the greater the detail. But there's a trade-off between the scale and usefulness. Somewhere around 1:25000 is a good scale for walking or hiking. For driving or riding a bike you might want 1:50000 and above to cover large distances.

3. Legend

Maps display key terrain features that help inform your decision-making process and route. After you've used topo maps for a while, you'll become familiar with what the contour lines represent in the real world – hills, saddles, valleys, ridges and depressions. On the map you'll also find the legend (or key). This is a graphical representation using symbols and colours to highlight features like roads, paths, railways, landmarks, natural features and vegetation.

Colours are generally standardised so green is used to represent vegetation – the darker the green the denser the vegetation. Blue is used to represent water – rivers, lakes, creeks. Some maps, like the Ordnance Survey 1:25000, include incredible detail, showing the type of vegetation, with separate icons representing coniferous forests and orchards.

The legend also provides important data for navigation (like declination) and a grid system that can be used to plot coordinates and pinpoint an exact location anywhere on the map.

Practising reading a map of your local area is a good way to develop your skills, and perhaps you'll find some interesting places worth investigating!

Using the sun

Let's say that you set off from your camp without a compass, map or phone reception in unfamiliar back-country (don't do this!). Maybe you're confident that even if you do get a little lost, you know enough about the local terrain to easily find your way back to camp. You climb up to the nearest escarpment and scrabble over some rocks. You pick up a trail heading over the ridgeline and into the next valley – what can go wrong? Half an hour later you realise that you are indeed a little lost. The trail has already split several times and now you want to head back and there are several choices. Which one will you take?

Noting the landmarks and terrain features you've passed, the direction you're travelling and the relative position of your camp can help you decide which path to take back. In this situation understanding the seasonal changes and the relative position of the sun's path throughout the day can help you find your direction.

Basic navigation using the sun is something everyone who ventures into the wilderness can benefit from. It can also be useful to double-check against the direction that your technology is sending you on. Smartphones can be wrong, and you might want to use the sun as a rough guide even if you have a map.

Ask most people which direction the sun travels in and they will most likely tell you that it 'rises in the east and sets in the west' but this is approximate and only accurate on two days of the year – the spring and autumn equinoxes.

This is because the Earth is tilted and different points in each hemisphere experience more or less sunlight at different times of the year as the Earth arcs around the sun, moving towards and away from the sun. Over a year this tilt results in more daylight hours in summer and less in winter.

Note that this will also depend on your latitude – how far north or south your position is on the Earth's surface. The closer to the North Pole the longer the days in summer and shorter in winter. This is reversed in the Southern Hemisphere.

The highest point of the sun in its arc across the sky will indicate that it's midday – the sun's midway point between sunset and sunrise. At midday the sun will always be due south, so if your back is to the sun you can bet you're facing north. In the Southern Hemisphere this works in reverse.

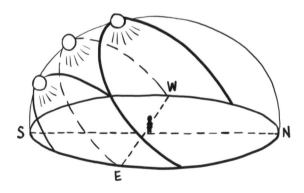

Geocaching and orienteering

GEOCACHING

Geocaching is a global treasure hunt where participants use GPS and a smartphone app, instead of a map, to hunt for buried treasure in the form of a 'cache'. I am not a massive tech head but I think geocaching is brilliant fun and an awesome way to develop observational skills while hiking or walking.

Invented in Oregon, United States in 2003, the first geocache was posted to a Usenet newsgroup. It was a partially buried bucket containing videos, books, some cash and, weirdly, a can of baked beans which has survived and is now a trackable item called the 'Original Can of Beans'!

Worldwide (except North Korea - boo!)

In my region, there are over 3500 caches and hundreds within 30km (18mi) of my house. There are over 3 million caches worldwide on every continent, including Antarctica. Geocaching is a goal-orientated game of discovery as you look for the hidden caches which can range from tiny (even nano) containers to larger waterproof ones. They usually contain a logbook for geocachers to record their visit and potentially a small treasure (aka swag)!

Some caches are extremely challenging to find and can be very remote, even requiring scuba gear, climbing equipment or a boat to reach them. The app gives you hints to their whereabouts and users can rate the difficulty, terrain and size of a cache.

Logging a cache

The idea is to collect the caches and their treasure, make a recording of the find in the logbook within the cache and online (or in the app) later. Logging the cache online lets the cache owner know that you've found it. You can leave notes on the condition of the cache and provide information for future geocachers about the area – no spoilers, though!

Collecting geo-swag

When taking a treasure as a souvenir you're encouraged to leave something of equal or greater value. Some items have special instructions and are supposed to be moved from cache to cache, others might contain specific educational notes or historic information about the area.

There are over 15 different official cache types which have various functions, including traditional cache, challenge cache (requires you to complete a task), night cache (supposed to be found at night), mystery cache (requires you to solve a puzzle or riddle) and CITO (cache in / trash out) cache (encourages you to go on litter clean-up in the local area!).

Geocaching for kids

For some families that struggle to get their kids outdoors, geocaching offers incentives to motivate more outings. What child doesn't like a treasure hunt? Having played geocaching with my kids, I can testify to how addictive it is. It has all the qualities kids tend to love – discovery, exploration and adventure. Plus it has several rewards – finding the cache, opening the container, exposing the contents, signing the logbook, and taking and exchanging a potential souvenir (or 'special treat' as my daughter likes to call it). It's fun and encourages the idea of thoughtfully swapping gifts with each other.

Afterwards, logging the find via the website gives a sense of completeness. It's also a chance for kids to use their recall abilities and creative writing skills.

The app has both a mapping and compass view, which can be a useful way to introduce them to the real thing later. The compass view has a countdown for distance which can be exciting for kids.

Geocaching for hiking and discovery

Geocaching is definitely a fun addition to a hike, and it can take you to places that you've never been, often remarkably beautiful locations only a local would know, or places that have a personal connection to the person who hid the cache.

It's this thoughtfulness from someone who you'll probably never meet that brings a special sense of connection to people and place through the gameplay. Some cities and regions have GeoTours, which is a clever way to guide visitors through historic sites and places of interest via a collection of geocaches (kids love GeoTours as they get multiple hunts!).

Community

There is a huge online community who arrange IRL (in real life) meet-ups. There are even 'event caches' that appear at specific times with coordinates of a gathering of local geocachers or geocaching organisations. Some of these meet-ups are in remote locations – like the middle of an Australian desert – and are a great way to meet fellow campers!

DIY

Perhaps one of the best features of geocaching is that you can be a participant as well as a creator. As long as you follow the geocache guidelines and can maintain the cache, there's nothing stopping you from creating your own geocache, adding your own personal touch to the contents, then hiding it in your favourite spot in nature. You simply upload the coordinates to geocaching.com. This is a wonderful way to share in the treasure of the cache, but also the beauty of your favourite spot!

What to take

Follow the advice from the 10 essentials (*see* p. 164). And be sure to have:

- [ ] a fully charged GPS or smartphone with extra batteries or a charging device
- [ ] a stick or hiking pole, which is useful for poking around in the undergrowth
- [ ] a torch (flashlight)
- [ ] swag to exchange – the golden rule is something of equal or higher value
- [ ] pencil or pen
- [ ] rubbish bag for collecting trash in the area.

ORIENTEERING

When I was growing up in the 1980s orienteering was *the* outdoor pursuit challenge for school kids as it encouraged teamwork and combined elements of land navigation using topographic maps and a compass. Teachers loved it as it incorporated the dreaded cross-country running that they enjoyed inflicting on us, while they slacked off and put their feet up (ha!).

Orienteering is a course that usually has a start, finish and various control or checkpoints that need to be visited in a particular order. Participants are given control descriptions (clue sheets) which describe the position of the control points using simple text or symbols.

Variations include scatter and score courses. Scatter courses allow participants to plan their own route to collect control points in any order. Score courses are time-limited and participants have to collect as many controls as possible within a specified time.

Traditionally, competitors are issued control cards. They use a ticket or needle punch that punches a pattern of small holes into the control card. Most events now use electronic punching with a device known as a dibber, e-stick or e-punch – an electronic timing device that straps to your finger. The code punch is verified proof that the contestant has visited the control point. The fastest person or team to complete the course is the winner.

Is there an app for that?

Of course there is! iOrienteering is a smartphone app that gives you all the tools you need to set up, manage and compete in your own event.

Reading the weather

'Rainbow in the morning, is a shepherd's warning; a rainbow at night is the shepherd's delight.'
– proverb

For our early ancestors, the observation, examination and attempt to forecast the weather would have been crucial for their day-to-day lives. Understanding the weather could mean the difference between life and death for a sailor, a successful quest for a hunter, a safe flock for a shepherd, or an exceptional crop for a farmer. Even today, it's so much a part of our lives and culture that many of us check the weather forecast each morning and then discuss the weather when we meet people throughout the day.

Attempting to forecast the weather is at least as old as written language itself. The ancient Babylonians had methods for predicting the weather, but it was the Greeks who created a system based on observation and the science of the time. The Greek philosopher Aristotle wrote a treatise in four books, called *Meteorology*, that described the properties of weather as the

interactions between the four elements – temperature (fire), air, water and earth. Meteorology is the name of the branch of science still used today to forecast weather.

UNDERSTANDING HOW THE WEATHER WORKS

Weather is simply the state of our atmosphere (both local and global) measured by observations of temperature, precipitation, wind speed and cloud formation.

Knowing a bit about how weather works and being able to read signs of changes in conditions can be important when camping and hiking, particularly if you're in remote areas with changeable conditions. You may need to prepare your campsite or other equipment accordingly and, in some instances, you may even need to plan for evacuation.

Knowing what you're in for shouldn't be confined to the latest information on an app. Weather conditions can change rapidly and sometimes even the best forecasts are unreliable. This is especially true in mountainous or coastal regions.

WIND

The wind comes in two major flavours – local and global. The local wind is shaped by your immediate surroundings and topology, and the global wind can bring major changes in weather.

Local wind

Local wind is created by the difference in temperature, usually between a body of water and a landmass or differences in height, like a mountain and valley. One mass is heating (or cooling) faster than the other, creating changes in air temperature and pressure.

Think of a sea breeze that comes from offshore in the afternoon. In Australia, the 'Fremantle Doctor' is a welcome afternoon sea breeze that comes from the Indian Ocean and cools Perth, Western

Australia during the height of summer. In the Midwestern United States, the much more threatening plough winds (also known as 'Derecho') are seasonal groups of fast-moving, straight-line storms that cause hurricane-force winds, tornadoes, heavy rains and flash floods.

Recognising the direction wind is coming from can be an indication of fair weather or foul. And learning the characteristics of local winds can be helpful in anticipating changing conditions.

Katabatic wind

Katabatic (from the Greek 'katabasis', meaning 'descending') wind is a general name given to a local wind that brings cold air from high mountain tops or glaciers down into the valley below, sometimes at high speeds. Katabatic winds are caused by rapidly cooling dense air that is pulled downwards by gravity, warming as it descends. In New Zealand, the Barber is an example of one such notorious wind that descends on the town of Greymouth on the west coast of the South Island.

Hikers and climbers, in particular, should pay attention to these types of winds. Plan your campsite accordingly as some of these winds can be extremely violent and unpredictable.

Global wind

Global or atmospheric weather systems (or weather fronts) are changes in temperature, precipitation, wind speed and cloud formation caused by changes in air pressure when two large systems with different characteristics meet and exchange heat and humidity. A cold front is an area of cold air replacing warm air, and vice versa. Major changes in frontal weather patterns are generally characterised by fast-moving cloud at various elevations. If clouds at different levels are moving in opposing directions and there are numerous varieties of clouds, this is a clue that bad weather is on its way.

READING CLOUDS

Perhaps one of the simplest and most fun ways to understand the weather is by identifying and interpreting cloud formations. It's also an enjoyable way to pass the time while outdoors! According to the United Kingdom's Met Office, there are at least 10 types of clouds that are divided into three categories depending on their shape, height and other characteristics.

As a general rule, the higher the cloud the less chance there will be rain. Cloud that is above 5500m (18,000ft) is considered high cloud and is mostly composed of ice crystals. Lower clouds are principally composed of water droplets, and so have the potential for rain.

The main groups are cirrus, stratus and cumulus.

Cirrus
High clouds, generally found above 5000m (16,500ft) made of ice crystals forming white, wispy streaks. Cirrus is a good indicator of fine weather.

Stratus

Stratus is a thick layer of uniform cloud produced when warm, moist air meets a colder layer. A dark blanket of stratus can mean rain or snow.

Cumulus

Cumulus is everyone's favourite fluffy cloud but it's also the most temperamental. They are best described as layered, globular rolls (their name is Latin for 'pile' or 'heap'). They range from the relatively harmless stratocumulus (little fluffy clouds) to the threatening cumulonimbus storm cloud.

CLOUD VARIATIONS

Clouds are further classified with a Latin prefix which identifies their height:

- Cirro: above 5000m (20,000ft)
- Alto: between 2000 and 5000m (6500 to 20,000ft)
- Nimbo (or nimbus): below 2000m (6500ft)

The mains clouds to be aware of when camping are clouds that produce rain or storm conditions.

Cirrostratus

Cirrostratus is a high-level cloud found between 5000m (16,000ft) to 12km (39,000ft). It's a hazy cloud formation that's generally uniform in nature and is hard to detect.

Cirrostratus can form a distinguished 'halo' around the sun and moon. It's where the old saying, 'A ring around the moon means rain soon' comes from, and is a reference to the cirrostratus halo effect indicating a warm front coming through, which could mean potential rain.

Cirrocumulus

Cirrocumulus is another high-level cloud found between approximately 6000m to 15km (19,500 to 50,000ft). Cirrocumulus is made up of small balls of globular fluffy clouds that light up at sunrise or sunset. If cirrocumulus forms with cirrostratus at the same time it usually means rain is coming.

Nimbostratus

Nimbostratus is a medium-low level cloud found below 3000m (9800ft). Its name comes from the Latin 'nimbus', meaning 'rainstorm'. It appears as a thick layer of grey and dark cloud that is almost uniform. Nimbostratus is likely to produce continuous and lasting rain (or snow and sleet) but generally no thunderstorms.

Altocumulus

Altocumulus is a middle-altitude cloud found between 2000 to 6000m. It's larger and darker than cirrocumulus and smaller than the low-level stratocumulus. Altocumulus is often located between the opposing cold and warm fronts. When found in its towering form, it likely means thunderstorms later in the day.

Altocumulus is one of the three warning clouds in aviation as it can develop into the ominous cumulonimbus.

Cumulonimbus

Cumulonimbus forms in low to high levels of 500 to 16,000m. It has extremely dense clouds that in its early stages develop into an enormous vertical tower resembling a cauliflower. When it's fully elevated, the top of the cloud begins to flatten (known as an 'anvil top'). The base of the cloud may be several kilometres (3 or more miles).

Mammatocumulus

Mammatocumulus is also known as mammatus or mamma. A mammatus consists of small bubble-like clouds that form at the base of the cumulonimbus tower. It indicates extreme weather ahead.

IDENTIFYING THUNDERSTORMS

Under normal conditions, the common cumulus humilis are known as 'fairweather cumulus' and have a limited vertical extent (height from base to top). But with changes in temperature, moisture and humidity cumulus clouds can start to extend vertically, first forming cumulus mediocris (moderate) and eventually forming the towering cumulus congestus.

Morning cumulus humilis clouds are a sign that this process will develop throughout the day, increasing in size and height in the late afternoon. Once they have formed a considerable height of approximately 10km (6mi), it's an indication that the atmosphere is becoming more unstable and these 'thunderheads' are likely to bring severe weather. At this stage rain is usually just a question of time and if the cloud is still developing vertically, the chances are it will transform into a thunderstorm – cumulonimbus.

When the tops of tall cumulonimbus start to become wispy and eventually flatten into an 'anvil top' it's a signal of an imminent thunderstorm. Lightning, hail or heavy rain with the potential for flash flooding and strong gale-force winds are likely.

If there's a cluster of cumulonimbus (called a 'supercell') or the appearance of mammatus you're in for trouble and a big storm.

Thunder and lightning

The precise underlying mechanics of lightning and thunder are still debated by scientists, but lightning is a phenomenon that mainly occurs in clouds when warm air is mixed with cooler air and an electrical transfer takes place between positively and negatively charged particles. This results in an intense electrical discharge.

Lightning creates a brilliant flash – sometimes a bolt – of supercharged light and heat (hotter than the surface of the sun!)

that comes either from within a cloud, from one cloud to another, or from a cloud to the ground. Lightning is usually almost immediately followed by thunder. A loud thunderclap indicates a cloud-to-ground strike, while a low sustained rumble of several seconds or more is likely to be a cloud-to-cloud strike.

The speed of light is faster than the speed of sound which is why lightning will always appear before thunder is heard. Almost everyone knows the trick of counting seconds between lightning and thunder to determine the distance you are from the storm. If that count starts decreasing, the storm is heading your way. For every five seconds you count between each strike, the storm will be 1.5km (0.93mi) away.

Storm preparation

Being caught in a severe or hurricane-level storm can be both scary and dangerous. I was once caught in hurricane Isidore while in Mérida, in the Mexican state of Yucatán. The storm was incredibly powerful, with buildings and vehicles being destroyed, trees and powerlines pulled from the ground and flooding over a huge area. We ended up living in a hotel room for 10 days with the toilet backing up (!) before being evacuating by the Mexican army (this was the first of two evacuations by the army on that trip!). Fortunately, we were in a solid building and had plenty of time to prepare.

The foreknowledge that a storm is on its way can save lives. If you find yourself with a severe incoming storm you need to prepare. Tune in to the radio or one of the many available weather apps which should give you a reliable forecast. Keep communication channels open – make sure your radio and mobile phone are charged. If possible, let friends, family or the park authorities know your whereabouts.

Reading the vital signs in the weather is a useful skill in these situations and may give you time to prepare for severe weather.

Start preparing your campsite by removing any dead standing trees and branches in the vicinity that might cause damage. Pack all non-essential equipment away into your vehicle or tent. Tie down any objects that can't be packed away. Ensure that your campfire is extinguished and gas bottles are safely turned to off.

Check that your tent and other structures are secured with stakes and pegs. Use extra guy ropes, tie downs or cable ties as necessary. If you have additional tarps (and time), put a tarp under your tent, making sure that the edges are not protruding out beyond the tent (otherwise this will encourage water to pool). You can use your vehicle as a windbreak, but make sure it's parked somewhere on high ground with drainage.

Consider where water run-off will occur around your camp and dig the appropriate trenches for draining water away.

Make sure you complete your outdoor preparation before you start inside your tent. Retrieve important gear in case of an emergency: warm clothing, torch (flashlight), lantern, first-aid kit, radio, mobile phone, gas burner, lighter (or fire kit), food, water bottle,

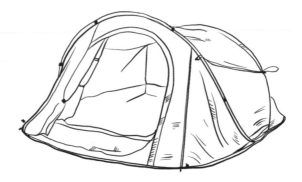

spare batteries, car keys, maps, multitool knife, cable ties, gaffa tape (handy for fixing a ripped tent), and anything else that will be useful during a prolonged storm, and will be helpful in an emergency situation. Pack your gear into dry bags or plastic bags if you have them.

Don't be tempted to cook food inside your tent during a storm even if you are set up for secure cooking (*see* p. 108) – it's too dangerous in volatile conditions. If you must have hot food or boil a billy, pitch a tarp low to the ground, opening on the leeward (downwind) side of the weather. This shelter will be your kitchen area.

Drowning from flash flooding claims more lives than any other weather-related disaster. This is why it's recommended to camp on elevated ground and well away from the banks of rivers or lakes. If you do need to evacuate your campsite, seek the highest ground possible and don't cross fast-flowing water, either on foot or in a car.

Avoiding lightning strikes

Having camped in Queensland, Australia during a storm front that produced nearly 30,000 lightning strikes, I can tell you that it's an awe-inspiring and somewhat disorienting experience (some campers nearby thought that we were being invaded by spacecraft!).

While it's relatively rare, globally, tens of thousands of people are struck by lightning each year, so being able to identify imminent danger from a storm can be lifesaving.

If you're in the path of a thunderstorm you should act with caution. The main advice for campers is not to seek shelter in your tent. You are safer in a car, provided you're not touching any metal as the metal frame of the vehicle will conduct electricity.

If there's a building nearby head for that as the wiring and drainage pipes will most likely conduct any electricity from a strike. Dense forest will provide some protection due to a large number of trees. If you find yourself in an exposed environment you should head for low ground as soon as possible.

Always:

- ☐ stay away from water
- ☐ avoid open areas and exposed hilltops
- ☐ move away from tall, isolated trees
- ☐ discard any metal objects, like walking or tent poles
- ☐ avoid lying flat on the ground – you're making yourself a larger target
- ☐ if you're in a group and not sheltered together, spread out to reduce the risk of a single target

If there's a thunderstorm overhead crouch as low as you can with the balls of your feet firmly planted on the ground. Hold your ankles.

There are some sure signs of a lightning striking close by that you can be alert to. If you smell a metallic chlorine odour (ozone), your hair starts to stand on end and there's a loud buzzing noise, move away quickly as there is sure to be a strike in your vicinity!

Stargazing

The universe is a big place! If you live in the city, the night sky probably doesn't demand much of your attention. As you go about your busy life you're absorbed by what's at hand, and the macrocosm is often taken for granted.

One of the great joys of a camping trip is that you're (ideally) away from light pollution where there's a good chance that you'll be exposed to the truly awe-inspiring presence of the cosmos. Having spent many nights camping in Australia, New Zealand and the United States where there's plenty of wilderness unpolluted by artificial light, it can be quite a shock to witness the unfathomable vastness of the Milky Way above. Stargazing is a reminder of our tiny part within a potentially infinite universe. For me, watching a starry sky is always a healthy reminder to take stock and appreciate life and the majesty of nature.

For most of human history, stargazing around a campfire would have been a regular night-time activity. Almost all cultures have some sort of belief system that explains the origins of the universe, the constellations and planets. The features of the heavens were incredibly important to our ancestors, not only for spiritual purposes and remembering their mythologies, but also as an essential tool for navigation.

NAVIGATING WITH THE STARS

While identifying constellations and planets is a fun skill to learn and the basis of a good campfire yarn, it also gives you some reassurance knowing that in the absence of modern technology you could find your way by the stars.

Here's a short guide to some popular constellations and asterisms (smaller group of stars within a constellation) and how they can help guide you. Depending on where you live – the Northern or Southern Hemisphere – you'll have a different view.

NORTHERN VERSUS SOUTHERN HEMISPHERES

From a human perspective, constellations always seem to be moving in the night sky depending on the time of year. This is because of the Earth's own orbit, and its orbit around the sun. The Earth's precession (axial tilt or 'wobble') also plays a part in how we view constellations, although this change is almost imperceptible during a human lifetime.

Because of this, each hemisphere has a different 'view' of the celestial dome and there are some constellations that are unique to the different hemispheres. These are called circumpolar constellations. Circumpolar constellations appear fixed and so can be used for navigation, and as signposts for finding other constellations. Not only is our view of the night sky determined by the Earth's relative position to the sun, but the area of sky we view is also determined by our latitude and longitude.

Basic constellations and star navigation for the Northern Hemisphere

Constellation: Ursa Major

Ursa Major (or Great Bear) is a large constellation that was well known to Palaeolithic hunters and plays a notable role in many cultures and mythologies around the world.

Ursa Major is probably most well-known for containing an asterism called the Big Dipper (aka Saucepan, Plough, Great Wagon).

The Big Dipper is a prominent group of seven bright stars that forms the shape of a ladle or saucepan. It's the most easily recognisable star pattern in the Northern Hemisphere and is usually where beginners start in their quest to learn about the night sky.

The Big Dipper is often called a guide (or signpost start) because it's used to find the position of other stars and constellations, including the most famous of navigation stars, Polaris (the North Star).

Constellation: Ursa Minor

Just like the Big Dipper, Ursa Minor contains a group of seven stars called the Little Dipper (or Little Bear) that also forms the shape of a ladle or saucepan. Although dimmer to the eye, the Little Dipper can also be used as a signpost for celestial navigation because the North Star is the last star on the Little Dipper's handle.

In spring and summer, constellations like the Big and Little Dippers are high overhead. In autumn and winter, they're found much closer towards the horizon. This is where the saying, 'spring up and fall down' comes from.

Star: Polaris

Also known as the North Star and the Pole Star, Polaris is a yellow-white supergiant star. It's the brightest visible star within Ursa Minor and one of the brightest stars visible to the naked eye in the Northern Hemisphere.

Polaris lies close to the north celestial pole and, because of its position in relation to the Earth's rotational axis, it appears to be almost fixed all year round. This is why it's known as the North Star and identifying it is so important for navigation. Once you use your signpost – like the Big and Little Dipper – to find Polaris, you'll have a fairly accurate fix on where north is. From there you can discover other constellations.

Constellation: Cassiopeia

Named after Queen Cassiopeia in Greek mythology, Cassiopeia is shaped like the letter 'W' and is easily visible with the naked eye. It's a constellation of five bright stars about the size of an outstretched hand.

Cassiopeia is a useful signpost for finding the North Star as it will always be directly opposite the Big Dipper, and therefore often high in the winter sky when the Big Dipper is at its lowest point on the horizon.

Asterism: Summer Triangle

The Summer Triangle consists of a collection of three bright stars, Vega, Altair and Deneb. It's visible in the north at any time of year – even under light pollution – but, as the name suggests, the Summer Triangle is most prominent in summer. For folk in the Northern Hemisphere, when the Summer Triangle starts to brighten it's a good sign that spring has turned and summer is coming.

In early summer, Vega is the brightest star found in the eastern sky and the brightest star in the triangle. Holding (or imagining) a ruler or stick of about 30cm (12in) at arm's length, with one end of the ruler obscuring Vega, you can plot a path to the right and down towards the horizon. Here you'll find another very bright star, Altair. If you look to the lower left of Vega, you'll find Daneb the third brightest star in the triangle.

Congratulations, you've spotted the Summer Triangle! In mid-summer the triangle will be high in the eastern sky and chances are you'll notice it almost every time you gaze towards the stars.

Constellation: Orion

Also known as The Hunter, Orion was well-known to our ancestors and first appears in recorded history in the Sumerian creation myths, like 'The Epic of Gilgamesh'. Egyptians, Babylonians and Aztecs all had Orion as an integral part of their myths. One theory about the Giza pyramids in Egypt is that they were built to align with the three stars of Orion's Belt.

Orion is one of the most easily recognisable constellations in the Northern Hemisphere and is also a key constellation for navigation. In winter, Orion takes the shape of a hunter with a bow and belt.

Looking for Orion's Belt is the easiest way to locate Orion in the night sky. Orion's Belt is an asterism (sometimes known as Celestial Bridge, Three Kings and Three Sisters) made up of three very bright stars – Alnitak, Alnilam and Mintaka.

Best viewed in the northern winter, Orion ascends towards the east in the early evening, moving across the night sky in a westerly direction through the night. Orion can be used to locate other stars. For instance, if you extend Orion's Belt to the south-east you'll locate Sirius, the Dog Star (brightest star in the night-time sky).

For countries in the Southern Hemisphere, Orion is viewed as the Pot or the Saucepan (*see* p. 215).

Basic constellations and star navigation for the Southern Hemisphere

Asterism: Southern Cross

In the Northern Hemisphere, the Big Dipper is the constellation that most people can name and find in the night sky, while in the Southern Hemisphere, it's the Crux Australis and its famous asterism, the Southern Cross.

The Southern Cross is made up of five stars which form an easily recognisable cross or kite shape. In southern parts of Australia, New Zealand, South Africa and Southern Chile, the Southern Cross appears fixed (circumpolar) in the night sky. The Cross' two brightest stars – Acrux and Gacrux – point the way to the southern celestial pole and so are useful in navigation for finding the south.

Star: Alpha Centauri

At only 4.37 light-years away, Alpha Centauri (or Alpha Cen) is the Earth's nearest neighbouring star and planetary system. Because of this it's on the spotting list of every serious stargazer. Alpha Cen appears as one star but it's actually two stars orbiting each other, what's known as a 'binary' system. Together they form the brightest star in the Centaurus constellation and the third brightest in the night sky.

To stargazers south of latitude 29°S (southern parts South Africa, Australia, New Zealand and South America) Alpha Centauri is circumpolar and so can be seen all year round.

Alpha Cen is one of two bright stars that form the Southern Pointers, another tool in your kit for navigation and finding true south.

Stars: Southern Pointers

The Southern Pointers consist of two stars – Alpha Centauri and the close by (in galactic terms) Beta Centauri, which are just 390 light-years from each other. Both stars are part of the constellation of Centaurus and are collectively known as the Southern Pointers, as they are associated with the Southern Cross.

Viewed from the south, you'll always find the Southern Pointers to the left of the Crux. They're a helpful signpost to confirm you have found the Southern Cross, and not the nearby False Cross. Like the Summer Triangle, once found they're not easily forgotten.

Constellation: Orion

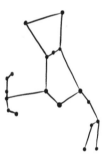

In the Southern Hemisphere, Orion is viewed 'upside down' when compared to the north and so takes on a different shape. In the south it's commonly known as the Pot or Saucepan. The three stars of Orion's Belt form the base of the pot, and the pot's handle is Orion's sword.

Coalsack Nebula (Emu in the Sky)

When looking south on a clear, moonless night in the Southern Hemisphere, you can find a dark interstellar cloud made up of dust and gas, known to many Indigenous peoples as the Emu in the Sky.

The cloud is a dark nebula and is a prominent feature. It's easy to find with the naked eye as it obscures the bright light from the Milky Way behind it. For some Indigenous peoples, the emu watches over them as a law-man, ensuring that they don't stray from their traditional laws.

TOOLS

Stargazing can become addictive, especially for kids when they start to recognise constellations. My daughter can't leave the house on a clear night without looking for the Southern Cross or Orion's pot.

To begin with there's no need to buy special tools. On a clear night away from the light of 'civilisation', there's plenty to see with the naked eye. You definitely don't need a telescope. But as you start to recognise more constellations you might want to add some tools to your kit. Binoculars are pretty handy. A lightweight 7x50 or 10x50 magnification which can attach to a camera tripod works well. A DSLR (digital single-lens reflex) camera lens mounted on a decent tripod will help you kickstart your astrophotography career.

Here are some helpful tools to consider:

☐ binoculars, monocular, telescope or spotting scope (portable high-power telescope)

☐ DSLR camera

☐ red light torch or flashlight (a torch that gives you red light to see by, while at the same time keeping your eyes adjusted for the dark)

☐ compass

☐ star maps and guides

☐ apps – Star Walk (iPhone) or Google Sky Map (Android)

For the best results you need to be away from any interfering light sources – that includes the campfire! Lying down and keeping warm with blankets and the appropriate clothing is the best way to enjoy the night sky. Give it 20 minutes and your eyes will adjust. Give it more time and the stars will really start to emerge.

Mindfulness in nature

'Rest in natural great peace.
This exhausted mind
Beaten helpless by karma and neurotic thought
Like the relentless fury of the pounding waves
In the infinite ocean of samsara.
Rest in natural great peace.'
– Nyoshul Khenpo Rinpoche

'Vis medicatrix natura (the healing power of nature).'
– Hippocrates

Some years ago I was lucky enough to spend nearly six months in Peru and Bolivia. A large part of the trip was spent deep in the Amazon rainforest with the opportunity to witness this incredible wilderness up close. Covering nearly 7 million km² (2.7 million mi²), the Amazon Basin is one of the world's most biodiverse environments. It holds 10 per cent of the world's native and endangered flora and fauna, so the opportunities for nature lovers are endless.

When not hiking, I lived in a basic one-room thatched hut on stilts. It was close to a small village but was completely off-grid, with no electricity or running water (except the stream below my hut!). Living on less than $1 (50p) a day was my idea of paradise. I had time on my hands to get into the rhythms of village life and spent most of my time idly wandering in the forest and observing nature. Looking back through the new lens of being a busy parent, this seems almost impossibly luxurious!

At first, the sound of the rainforest (especially at night – predators and prey are awake) was actually quite intense. It's a complex wall of sound with its own mysterious rhythm created by a multitude of insects, frogs, bats, birds and monkeys all working together in unison to create a grand symphony of hypnotic and atmospheric soundscapes. After a while, as the brain adjusts, you develop the ability to separate the layers and identify the patterns of the song from each creature.

After getting over any initial concerns about predators and biting insects (of which there are many!) the jungle is a comfortable and welcoming environment with an average day and night-time temperature hovering around a perfect 25°C. It's a womb-like environment where you can easily relax and study the incredible biodiversity around you.

I began to find low-light spots where the sun broke through the high canopy and I could comfortably sit to witness the sights and sounds of the jungle. Using some basic meditation techniques that I'd learned as a kid, I found I could happily spend hours in these spaces in an untroubled (apart from the odd insect bite) meditative state.

Little did I know that I was practising forest bathing. Known as 'shinrin-yoku' in Japan, it's roughly translated as 'making contact and taking in the atmosphere of the forest'. Shinrin-yoku is a formal therapy technique inspired by Shinto reverence for nature, focusing on the health benefits of time spent in the forest.

According to Japanese studies, there are many positive health benefits from forest bathing, like significantly reducing blood pressure and cortisol levels, as well as enhancing mood and mental wellness, and reducing depression and anxiety. Forest bathing is linked with boosting the immune system, and scientists think that this is partly an effect from contact with phytoncides (essential oils) released from trees that act to boost the human immune function.

According to the attention restoration theory (ART) developed by Rachel and Stephen Kaplan in the 1980s, spending time in an unthreatening natural environment can have a restorative effect because it can replenish depleted 'attentional resources'. Natural environments teem with 'soft fascinations' which stimulate us but require no effort from our attention.

Observing the rich and colourful textures of a forest or field of flowers, watching patterns in cloud formations, listening to a flowing river or bird song, and witnessing a sunrise or sunset are all soft fascinations. Scientists believe that there is something in these natural scenes that causes electrochemical changes in the brain which can lead people to enter a beneficial state of effortless attention.

Countless other scientific studies have built on the Kaplans' attention restoration theory and Japan's therapeutical shinrin-yoku to show that intentional time spent in nature offers huge physical and psychological upsides. It's already widely believed in many cultures that nature connection has a hidden healing hand that can be used as a channel to wellness. Now science is catching up with an explanation of how this works.

I left the Amazon fully restored, in much better physical and mental condition than when I arrived. Looking back, I can now see that my life has been made up of a series of chapters that have fluctuated between stressful urban periods and retreats back into nature. Without doubt, my subconscious recognised the antidote to any problem and found the remedy!

What is clear is that mindfulness in nature is not some sort of mystical juju. It's a practice that can have a tangible and measurable impact on health and wellbeing. While I'm no expert, this is my approach to mindfulness in nature which is straightforward and accessible to anyone. I hope you get a chance to try it.

PRACTISING MINDFULNESS MEDITATION IN NATURE

Perhaps the hardest thing about communicating mindfulness meditation is describing techniques and expected results. Personally, I think the best advice is not to pressure yourself with goals. Just practise a few different techniques and find out what works for you.

What to take

When was the last time you left home without your phone? What is the first thing you do in the morning? If your initial thought is to reach for your phone or computer, chances are you're suffering from attention theft. Despite being useful tools, digital devices are designed to encourage continual use by sending notifications with 'helpful' content or messages.

The first rule of mindfulness is to remove unwanted distractions. Leave your phone at home or in your car. Instead, take a day pack which should include some or all of the 10 essentials (*see* p. 164).

Choose your location

Personally, I believe mindfulness is an adventure best done solo, but you should always embark on your journey in a safe environment, preferably somewhere that you know well. It will ideally be in the wild, but it could be a local park or reserve to begin with. Make sure it's somewhere that you won't get lost, and where you'll be secure while you're in a relaxed state of being.

Mindful walk

First of all, it makes sense to spend some time in the area where you plan to meditate. A mindful walk is the best way to lead to a deeper experience. If the terrain is suitable, barefoot is the way to go. Let your feet sink into the ground and notice the feeling of grass and earth underfoot. During your walk pay attention to the details of the plant life surrounding you and begin to engage all of your five senses.

The five senses

One of the techniques of forest bathing is to engage the five senses – sight, sound, touch, smell and taste. This will help you connect with your surroundings. Notice the way the sunlight falls through the canopy, feel the texture of tree bark, tune into the sounds of the forest, rub leaves or flowers and inhale their fragrance, and take deep breaths to trigger your sense of smell – after a while, you will begin to taste the forest (yum)!

Find your spot

For me, this is simply finding a spot where I feel the most comfortable. If you're in a coniferous forest it's easy to find a comfortable place among the pine-needle litter. Your spot might be under a favourite tree, a wide-open space with a view, or a more enclosed area. If it's your first time, try a few different spots until you find one that feels the most comfortable. Check the area where you plan to relax – there's little point in meditating on a grass verge where you can roll downhill, or positioning yourself next to an ants' nest!

Relax man

Sit cross-legged or lie down. Close your eyes and begin to focus on your body. I like to start from my toes and move all the way up to the top of my head, consciously relaxing the muscles as I go. It helps to feel the weight of your body and the gravity pulling you down towards the ground. You will begin to notice how your body is touching and connecting with the earth beneath. Once you are feeling relaxed bring your attention to your breath.

Start with the breath

With your tongue gently resting on the roof of your mouth, start by breathing normally through your nose. Instead of raising your chest, use the inhale to compress your lower belly and the exhale to raise your belly. Begin to breath deeper and for longer, pausing for a second at the extent of the inhale and exhale. I like to use my imagination to visualise the diaphragm moving to the breath, delivering oxygen to my bloodstream!

Let it go

Once you're relaxed and breathing deeply, you'll begin tuning into the sounds surrounding you in the forest. Again, observe the sounds and smells but try to not to be drawn into actively analysing them.

You will notice that your mind begins to wander, triggering a cascade of thoughts, possibly questioning everything you're doing! You might start to focus on bodily sensations, convincing yourself you're uncomfortable or in pain. You might begin daydreaming about the past or what's happening in your life at the moment.

This 'thought invasion' is completely natural. The idea with mindfulness is to allow thoughts to happen but release them just as quickly as they arrive. A way to dismiss your thoughts is to gently bring your attention back to your breath. You're attempting to achieve an alert presence that endures moment to moment without the distraction of the mind's internal dialogue!

Bring it back

Try to remain like this for five minutes (you can go longer the more you do it). Each time your thoughts take you away, return to the breath. It's a good practice to slowly draw yourself out of meditation by partially opening your eyes, then slowly becoming aware of your body, and then your surroundings.

Welcome back

Well done! There's no right or wrong with mindfulness meditation, just practice!

Give thanks

Finally, Santosha is one of the eight yogic rules and translates as a kind of contentment in accepting and appreciating our life and condition. There are similar concepts in Christianity, and probably all other spiritual or religious practices. It might sound cheesy, but even if you aren't religious or 'spiritual', silently giving thanks to the Earth and our natural environment is a small but powerful gesture. After all, nature and our fellow plant and animal life gives us everything that we need to survive and thrive – food, water, medicine, materials for shelter and clothing, even the oxygen we breathe. It makes sense to acknowledge this and appreciate what a wonderful gift life is.

Resources

FURTHER READING

The Camper's Handbook, Thomas Hiram Holding, 1908
The Book of Camping and Woodcraft, Horace Kephart, 1910
How to Stay Alive in the Woods, Bradford Angier, 2001,
    Little Brown
How to Survive Your First Trip in the Wild, Paul de Magnanti, 2019,
    Rockridge Press
Field Guide to Wilderness Medicine 5th Edition, Paul S. Auerbach,
    2019, Elsevier
Bushcraft: A Family Guide, John Boe and Owen Senior, 2015, Vie
Bushcraft 101, Dave Canterbury, 2014, Adams Media
The Old Ways: A Journey on Foot, Robert Macfarlane, 2013,
    Penguin Press
The Wild Places, Robert Macfarlane, 2018, Granta
Wild Signs and Star Paths, Tristan Gooley, 2019, Sceptre
The Natural Explorer, Tristan Gooley, 2013, Hodder & Stoughton
How to Read the Weather, Storm Dunlop, 2018, Pavilion Books
A Camper's Guide to Weather Signs, Various, 2011, Read Books
Mallmann on Fire, Francis Mallmann, 2014, Workman
Wild Adventure Cookbook, Sarah Glover, 2018, Prestel

WEBSITES

homecamp.com.au
sectionhiker.com
modernhiker.com
weareexplorers.co
thehikinglife.com
theadventurejunkies.com
bushwalkingmanual.org.au
geocaching.com
lnt.org

APPS

AllTrails
Hikingproject
ViewRanger
The Outbound
Roadtrippers
Gaia GPS
Avenza Maps
Fatmap
Star Walk 2

Index

About the author

In 2014, **Doron Francis** and his wife Stephanie launched Homecamp, an outdoor lifestyle brand that aims to inspire people to get out and experience nature as much as possible. Homecamp has since built up a legion of loyal followers and customers who want to enjoy the outdoors, equipped with products and skills that will last a lifetime. Doron lives in Victoria, Australia with Stephanie and their three kids, and goes out in nature as often as he can. This is his second book for keen campers, following their first book, *Homecamp* (Hardie Grant, 2017).

Photo credits:

p. ii Forrest Mankins; pp. viii–1 Stefan Haworth; p. 6 Jess Abraham; pp. 8–9 Wild Road Wanderers; p. 25 Nick Anders; pp. 26–27 Wild Road Wanderers; p. 61 Adam Gibson; pp. 92–93 Doron Francis; p. 107 Brad Willets; p. 108 David Wilkinson; pp. 112–113 Stefan Haworth; p. 128 Brad Willets; p. 155 Padraig Croke; pp. 156–157 Greg Rosenke/Unsplash; p. 172 Padraig Croke; p. 197 Brad Willets; p. 231 Hilary Walker.

Published in 2021 by Hardie Grant Travel, a division of Hardie Grant Publishing

Hardie Grant Travel (Melbourne)
Building 1, 658 Church Street
Richmond, Victoria 3121

Hardie Grant Travel (Sydney)
Level 7, 45 Jones Street
Ultimo, NSW 2007

www.hardiegrant.com/au/travel

A catalogue record for this book is available from the National Library of Australia

NATIONAL
LIBRARY
OF AUSTRALIA

Hardie Grant acknowledges the Traditional Owners of the country on which we work, the Wurundjeri people of the Kulin nation and the Gadigal people of the Eora nation, and recognises their continuing connection to the land, waters and culture. We pay our respects to their Elders past, present and emerging.

Tent Life
ISBN 9781741177213

10 9 8 7 6 5 4 3 2 1

Publisher: Melissa Kayser
Project editor: Megan Cuthbert
Editor: Irma Gold
Proofreader: Rosanna Dutson
Design: Kåre Martens, HANDVERK

Research and writing assistance:
  Stephanie Francis
Typesetting: Megan Ellis
Index: Max McMaster

Colour reproduction by Megan Ellis and Splitting Image Colour Studio

Printed and bound in China by LEO Paper Products LTD.